FENTRESS BRADBURN ARCHITECTS

They that dig foundations deep,
Fit for realms to rise upon,
Little honor do they reap
Of their generation,
Any more than mountains gain
Stature till we reach the plain....

—Rudyard Kipling

FENTRESS BRADBURN ARCHITECTS

ROGER A. CHANDLER

Introduction by David Gebhard

Studio Press

WASHINGTON, D.C.

First published in the United States in 1995 by Studio Press,
an imprint of the American Institute of Architects, Washington, D.C.

Library of Congress Cataloging in Publication Data
Chandler, Roger A.
    Fentress Bradburn architects / introduction by David Gebhard.
        p.   cm.
      ISBN 1-55835-146-9 (cloth)
      1. Fentress, C. W.—Criticism and interpretation.   2. Bradburn, J.
    H.—Criticism and interpretation.   3. C.W. Fentress J.H. Bradburn
    and Associates.   I. Title.
    NA737.F45C48   1996
    720'.92'2—dc20   95-45336
                                                                          CIP
Designed by Abigail Sturges
Copy edited by Dr. Lois Nesbitt
Set in type by Mikes House
Printed and bound in Hong Kong
through Palace Press International, San Francisco

Jacket illustration:
Denver International Airport passenger terminal complex
Timothy Hursley, photographer

To Charlie, Michael, and Julian,
the next generation

C.W.F. and R.A.C.

CONTENTS

PREFACE

Dr. Roger A. Chandler

In late 1990 I was introduced to a young architect by a mutual friend. It was clear to me at our first encounter that this fellow had a definite sense of purpose and direction. His architecture had given that purpose meaning, but he was searching for a way to blueprint his direction intellectually without holding philosophical dialectics on the job site to prove his point. As much as we art historians like to lecture to the glare of two-dimensional images on a flat surface in a darkened classroom, architecture is profoundly more than that. It must, by its very nature, be experienced, touched, felt, probed, and prodded. Architecture influences the senses like no other art, and sometimes photographs alone will not do. Architecture must be conveyed through the view of its creator. Curt Fentress intuitively understood this. I proposed to help him translate his philosophies into book form. He really didn't need me to. Our recurring discussions of contemporary architectural issues convinced me that he was more than capable of accomplishing the task at hand. However, staring the completion of the Denver International Airport project squarely in the face while running a practice burgeoning under international interest in the airport venture convinced him to let me undertake the project. Fortunately for me Curt had long since defined his reasons and motivations for making, and I had only to bring that impetus to textual life. My friendship with Jim Bradburn evolved out of this project.

Jim, like his mentor John Dinkeloo, is an introspective fellow, not much given to publicity and skeptical about action that would put him in the spotlight. For Jim, such activity gets in the way of architecture and detracts from the poetic necessary to create good buildings. I can't say that I totally disagree with him, but I coaxed him into the project anyway. As I got to know him better, I recognized his creative genius. "Never underestimate the power of the right idea," he once said.

Part of the excitement I experience as a casual observer of this architectural team, now incorporated as C.W. Fentress J.H. Bradburn and Associates, derives from the fact that Jim is a technological virtuoso—the kind of architectural engineer who so baffles his competition that they often take shots at his work because they simply can't understand it. Ask him about any project, and his eyes light up with excitement. Most likely he won't say much, but you know from what he does say that there are new technologies in the offing and new creations about to be born. Which brings me back to getting shot at.

Like most firms that assume the challenge of public projects, Fentress Bradburn has taken its share of criticism. These designers willingly seize the responsibility for obviously controversial projects. They deliberately seek out such work. Admittedly this determination entails a certain amount of political risk, but to Curt and Jim the desire to design in the public forum far outweighs any hypothetical danger. They also believe that they can actually do something about public architecture as it has evolved in the late twentieth century. Instead of firing glancing critiques at bad buildings, they choose to act. Very determined, these fellows, and genuinely motivated to better their environment.

To my friends Curt and Jim, thank you for the opportunity to document the birth of what I believe is rapidly becoming a firm to be reckoned with on an international scale.

To my other colleagues who helped with the actual construction of this project, I must give special recognition. All have become friends and have contributed a great deal to the success of this volume. To Mike Wisneski, Thom Walsh, Brian Ostler, and Jan Gustafson, thanks for the humor. Lucidity is a precious thing during long and tedious exercises, and you folks kept me sane. To my personal research assistants Susan Guinn-Chipman and Mark T. Harpe, thank you. This work could not have been completed without your diligence. To the architects on the team that I consulted for factual details, Ron Booth, Chris Carvell, Brian Chaffee, Barbara Hochstetler, Mike Gengler, Jim Hartman, Art Hoy, John Kudrycki, Gary Morris, Jack Mousseau, John Salisbury, Mark Wagner, Thom Walsh, Mike Winters, and Mike Wisneski, thanks for the prompt assistance. (You owe me a pair of new shoes to replace those I wore out trying to chase you down for information.) To Rick Burkett, thanks for the great quote. To researchers Carol Carr, Jayne Coburn, Cydney Fisher, June Huhn, Lisa Jelliffe, and Kristin Wehrli, your assistance was incalculable, as was the work of writers Karen Gilbert, John Gossett, Sue Blosten, Deborah Chelemes, and Michel Pariseau. Superb technical support was provided by Minh Nguyen, Dan Monger, Susan Pratt, Mark McGlothlin, Nina Bazian, Michelle Ray, Renee Major, Dave Tompkins, and Marilyn White. To my newest friends and sterling New Yorkers, copy editor Dr. Lois Nesbitt, architect and critic G. Daniel Perry, and designer Abigail Sturges, you do excellent work. It has been a pleasure.

A very special thank you must go to my dear friend and mentor Professor David Gebhard for agreeing to take time out of his monumentally busy schedule to analyze the work in progress and address it in the intoduction.

Finally I would like to thank my wife, Gail, who once pointed out the value of such an exercise and who, in the face of my increasing preoccupation with other projects and lack of time spent with my family, saw this undertaking to its successful conclusion with encouragement and no complaints.

Denver, Colorado, 1994

INTRODUCTION

International Regionalism in Context

David Gebhard

Frontispiece. New Seoul Metropolitan Airport, Seoul, Korea. C.W. Fentress J.H. Bradburn and Associates, 1992.

Above. Chunghwamun Gate, Tŏksugung Palace, Seoul, Korea

Since the late 1960s architects, clients, and the public have become increasingly concerned with contextualism—the way in which a building, a garden, or an urban scheme may enhance the sense of specific geographic place. The ability to suggest a special sense of place can be accomplished in two ways. Designers may look at and respond to the individual environmental qualities of a region or locale, its climate and its geography, and then reflect these qualities in their buildings or landscapes. The other approach, often coupled with a sensitivity to environmental issues, seeks out the unique architectural history of a place. Has a specific architectural/landscape tradition evolved over the years that is readable to all? If so, designers have the opportunity to reflect these qualities in their designs.

The reasons for this quite recent development of contextualism are complex. To begin with, it signals an unquestionable reaction against the growing homogeneity of cities worldwide. Why bother to travel to China or Turkey, if these places look like one's own home? Compounding the sameness in the architecture, landscape, and planning of cities around the world is the general dullness of late modernist architecture coupled with a disturbing tendency to ignore the older scale of a place by erecting grandiose megastructures (especially, of course, skyscrapers or, as they are more fittingly labeled these days, high rises). Most people find these modernist additions to cities monotonously similar and downright unfriendly to human activities.

In observing the two-thousand-plus years of the Western European architectural tradition, one quickly sees that our concern for context is relatively recent. While some earlier buildings reflect specific environments, Western European architecture has at any given moment generally adhered to an "international" style. While the siting of an English Gothic cathedral in what amounted to a suburban location is unquestionably different from that of an urban French cathedral, these two designs exhibit many more shared design features than differences (figs. 1, 2). The rediscovery of Roman classicism as first expressed in the buildings of fifteenth-century Renaissance Italy spread in the following centuries throughout Europe. An early eighteenth-century architect in England was more interested in how his interpretation of the classical tradition related to that of Parisian and above all Roman designers than in whether it expressed a particular English quality (fig. 3).

It wasn't until the early nineteenth century that contextualism began to affect architectural imagery. Many factors contributed to this developing interest in evoking a sense of place. One was certainly the European architect's expanded understanding of world architecture (concurrent with the development in the late eighteenth century of the study of history as we know it today). It quickly became apparent that Europe's architectural tradition was simply one of many, each of which had its own validity. Even more important for contextualism was the growth of nationalism in the nineteenth century. The design of buildings, gardens, and the urban landscape became one way of expressing the nation-state. Predictably, nineteenth-century contextualism had more to do with myth of regions and of the nation-state than with historical fact. As composer Richard Wagner exemplified in his famed operas, myth realized through art was often far more effective in evoking nationalism than was history.

1. Cathedral, Wells, England, 1175–1239. Facade
2. Cathedral, Reims, France, 1211–60. Facade
3. Chiswick House, London, England, Earl of Burlington. Facade begun 1725
4. Stevens' House, Portland, Maine. J. C. Stevens, 1887
5. Bourne House, San Francisco, California. Willis K. Polk, 1895–96
6. McKlintock House, Palm Beach, Florida. Marion Sims Wyeth, 1923–29

7. Young House, Pasadena, California. George Washington Smith, 1927
8. Conkey House, Santa Fe, New Mexico. John Gaw Meem, 1928
9. Lovell House, Los Angeles, California. Richard J. Neutra, 1929
10. Civic Center Plan, Denver, Colorado. Edward Bennett, 1917

In the United States self-conscious contextualism did not enter the scene until the very end of the nineteenth century. The nationalist architecture that emerged after the 1876 Centennial Exhibition in Philadelphia reflected the East Coast Anglo-colonial tradition. By the mid-1890s colonial revival buildings and houses appeared from New England to California. The universalism of this single image was eventually challenged in a few areas by exotic regionalist imagery: the Spanish/Mediterranean in Florida, the mission revival in California, and the Pueblo or Santa Fe style in the Southwest (figs. 4–9).

Though the Anglo-colonial revival and other regionalist styles asserted themselves with appreciable creative strength during the first four decades of this century, they were constantly challenged by internationalist traditions ranging from Parisian Beaux-Arts classicism to the art deco/streamline moderne, and finally to International Style modernism. Certainly, from the early 1900s to the present, American architecture has committed above all to an international rather than a national or regional image.

Although early International Style modernism was supposedly concerned with the relationship of the building to its specific environment, it quickly became, as Henry-Russell Hitchcock and Philip Johnson announced in 1932, an architectural style, not an approach to a design problem. Like an automobile or an airplane of the time, the modernist building was designed as a machine (again, more in image than in fact) and could be erected in the tropics as easily as in the temperate zone.

Contextualism's slow return began in the late 1960s with the advent of the environmental movement. Environmentalists asserted that buildings should be designed first of all to respond to climatic conditions and then to other physical characteristics of their location. Buildings, they went on to assert, should be "responsible," they should reflect a concern for the world's limited materials and energy. Since precedent is always needed, many environmentalists turned back to a pre-1900 rural world that was antiurban and rustic and motivated by a do-it-yourself spirit.

In the nouveau-riche decades of the late 1970s and 1980s, the urgency of environmental issues in contextual architecture tended to be relegated to the sidelines. Instead contextualists found themselves entangled in a nostalgia for the past: wanting either to preserve older buildings and streetscapes or to exploit historic images. In the East and Midwest the always popular Anglo-colonial revival reasserted itself (now it even has its own middle-class magazine, *The Colonial Home*). In the Southwest, the older adobe revival was enthusiastically reanimated, and in California, the Spanish/Mediterranean tradition of the 1920s became the desired image for the opulent, oversized, architect-designed houses and tract spec housing.

For large-scale commercial, institutional, and governmental buildings a strange mixture of classicism and art deco became the norm among many postmodern designers. Other postmodernists who rejected direct references to the past secretly engaged in their own plagiarism of the past, mining the machine aesthetic of the 1920s avant-garde art and architecture (cubism, dadaism, expressionism, and surrealism). A version of modernism itself continued alongside postmodernism, but no longer possessed the creative force that had driven it in the 1950s and sixties. Late twentieth-century modernist designs more often than not reveal a fascination with pristine geometric volumes, especially shapes derived from such forms as the triangle or cylinder. This generally high-tech work delights in thin, shimmering skins of metal and glass (or stone, cut paper thin to read as a pure industrial product).

With only a handful of exceptions, postmodernist and late modernist designs turned their backs on environmental concerns, returning to anticontextual international imagery rather than expressing anything about their specific historical or geographic locales.

With the exception of a frontier version of the Hispanic tradition in the extreme southern section of Colorado, the buildings, landscape designs, and urban plans within the state essentially mirrored what was going on elsewhere in the United States. Up until the early 1900s Colorado clients and their architects transplanted images of the Northwest and Midwest to the plains, mountains, and western slope of the state in an effort to show that they were in no way provincial. When the economy had developed sufficiently, the earlier log structures were replaced by "correct" versions of the Italianate, Eastlake, Queen Anne, Richardsonian Romanesque, and Anglo-colonial revival.

Since 1900 a division has appeared between the desire to be a part of the national/international scene and the urge to suggest that Colorado is not New York or Illinois. Denver's turn-of-the-century City Beautiful planning schemes and projects for a state and city civic center were purely national, not regional (fig. 10). In contrast, a number of local and national architects turned to the then popular Mediterranean/Spanish colonial revival as a possible expression of the region. Historical myth might just have worked in the southern part of the state, but it was not convincing on the open plains and in the rugged mountains. Nonetheless, such buildings as McLaren and Hetherington's Pauline Roman Catholic Chapel at Colorado Springs and Day and Klauder's design for the University of Colorado at Boulder proved impressive essays in the Mediterranean tradition (figs. 11, 12).

By the 1930s thoughts of developing a regionalist architecture for Colorado had been pretty well abandoned (a notable exception was John Gaw Meem's 1937 Colorado Springs Fine Arts Center [fig. 13]). Except for cladding houses in brick, there certainly was nothing regional about Denver's acres of post-World War II spec housing. The city's principal large-scaled modernist buildings constructed after 1945 were meant to be experienced within the context of the American rather than the regional scene. They were stylistically and structurally international: they could have been built, with no changes, anywhere in the world.

With the breakup of the International Style ideological and design monopoly in the late 1960s, a few voices once again advocated some form of contextual regionalism in Colorado. The theme of regionalism provided a guise for preserving the artifacts (buildings) of the past through private and public historic preservation. Regionalism could also be realized through cultivating a set of rustic, informal images associated with nineteenth-century vernacular architecture (especially

5

6

7

8

9

10

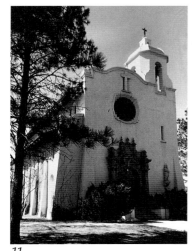

11

12

15

16

13

17

14

18

19

20

that encountered within the central mountain region). This form of contextualism (which often embraced environmental issues as well) worked within the confines of smaller towns and with small to modest-sized buildings but seemed inapplicable to large high-rise buildings.

Since the 1980s, several architects and architectural firms across the country have consciously tried to play the very difficult game of designing buildings that read as both national/international and contextual. Among them is the Colorado firm of C.W. Fentress J.H. Bradburn and Associates. The firm's early work is essentially national/international modernist. These buildings are finely detailed machines with skins that effectively define pristine geometric volumes.

As did other architects of the time, Fentress Bradburn enriched their late-eighties design palette by producing buildings that could certainly be labeled postmodern. In the Jefferson County Courts and Administration Building (1992), the architects evoked classical forms and then detailed the building as if it were a fine machine (fig. 14). Like their modernist work, Fentress Bradburn's skillful postmodern designs are essentially nonregionalist.

Responding to a variety of issues, the firm became increasingly involved with the question of regional contextualism. Fentress Bradburn's 1982 remodeling and restoration of the historic Kittredge Building (1881) in downtown Denver introduced the architects not only to the world of historic preservation but to the need to accommodate modernist ideals within historic forms (fig. 15). As the program required, their project for the Gemmill Mathematics Library and Engineering Sciences Building at the University of Colorado at Boulder (1992), a stone-sheathed Mediterranean building, uses the vocabulary established in the teens by the original Philadelphia architects, Day and Klauder (fig. 16).

Fentress Bradburn's design for the Denver International Airport's Passenger Terminal Complex (1993–94) is one of the major contemporary contributions to contextual regionalism in the United States. High-tech rules, but in this case the gleaming white-fabric "tents" (made of Teflon-coated fiberglass membrane) convincingly mirror the snowcapped peaks of the Rocky Mountains in the distance (fig. 17). Inside, the shape and above all the light penetrating through the fabric suggest the interior of a Plains Indian tepee. The game of suggesting regional context via abstract means is fascinating. One can never be sure, however, that such contextualism will be legible to the average person without written captions.

Reinforcing the building's abstract references to the region are a number of artworks that allude to the place. Especially effective, indicating a close rapport between architect and artist, is Patty Ortiz's *Experimental Aviation*: 140 birdlike airplanes suspended in front of a sandstone wall (designed by Barbara Hochstetler) whose profile hints at a silhouette of the Rocky Mountains (fig. 18). David Gregg's abstraction of a western mining railroad in *Dual Meridian* and Michael Singer's impressive untitled interior garden that recalls a pre-Columbian ruin from Mexico or Central America also address the region (figs. 19, 20).

Other recent Fentress Bradburn designs that explore contextualism are the Natural Resources Building in Olympia,

Washington (1992) and the National Wildlife Art Museum in Jackson Hole, Wyoming (1993–94). The New Denver International Airport and these last two projects suggest that a sense of region can be conveyed using a national/international architectural language based in machine imagery and the geometry of pure forms. Now that Fentress Bradburn has emerged on the international scene, designing major projects in such places as Korea and Thailand, the difficult task facing the firm will be to discover and then express in architecture the individual character of each new locale.

11. *Pauline Roman Catholic Chapel, Colorado Springs, Colorado. Thomas McLaren, 1920*
12. *University of Colorado at Boulder, Boulder, Colorado. Day and Klauder, 1919*
13. *Colorado Springs Fine Arts Center, Colorado Springs, Colorado. John Gaw Meem, 1937*
14. *Jefferson County Government Center, Courts and Administration Building, Golden, Colorado. C.W. Fentress J.H. Bradburn and Associates, 1993*
15. *Kittredge Building, Denver, Colorado. A. Morris Stuckert, 1881, restored by C.W. Fentress and Associates, 1980*
16. *Gemmill Mathematics Library and Engineering Sciences Building, University of Colorado at Boulder, Boulder, Colorado. C.W. Fentress J.H. Bradburn and Associates, 1992*
17. *Denver International Airport Passenger Terminal Complex, Denver, Colorado. C.W. Fentress J.H. Bradburn and Associates, 1994*
18. *Patty Ortiz*, Experimental Aviation, *1993–94*
19. *David Gregg*, Dual Meridian, *1993–94*
20. *Michael Singer*, Untitled, *1993–94*

CHAPTER ONE
The Architects in Context

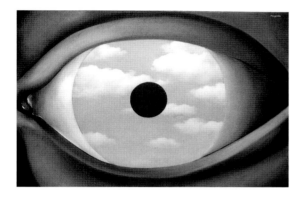

Frontispiece. 116 Inverness Drive East, Englewood, Colorado. C.W. Fentress and Associates, 1982

Above. René Magritte, The False Mirror, *1928, 21^{1}⁄₄ × 37⅛" (54 × 80.9 cm). Oil on canvas. Museum of Modern Art. Purchase*

Successful styles today have more enemies than friends. This ironic situation increases with growing stylistic choice, the consequence of a contentious pluralism which is to be welcomed until it results in a reactionary compromise, or the safe, bland building which appeals to planning committees and no-one else. If values and tastes do radically differ, then democratic politics must allow them expression and realization. The urban results will not be harmonious as a whole, except in small communities, but then who really wants to live in a city of one style, of one age and dimensionality?—Charles Jencks[1]

The essence of this pluralist dialogue first appeared in the politics of American architectural practice through the force of two dynamic wills. In this debate, all else was peripheral. Two voices shaped architecture as we have come to understand it. Both were innovators, both appropriators, but their ideals converged from disparate directions.

Consistently challenging colleagues on architecture of artistic merit, Louis Henri Sullivan believed American architecture to be an art form, arguing that "form follows function" (figs. 1, 2). Sullivan presented the independent architectural monument in both functionalist and prototypical formalist ways, both design ideas which influenced the modernist debate, and introduced Frank Lloyd Wright. Daniel H. Burnham, Sullivan's sometime friend and benefactor, did things another way (fig. 3). Burnham's projects, no matter how great or small, assumed a grandeur often unmatched in his day. He was the first to express William Le Baron Jenny's invention of the completely steel structural frame. Burnham built the first building recognized by the popular press as a skyscraper (fig. 4). He also developed the prototypical architectural practice as a big business in the public forum through political connections. Burnham pressed for the comprehensive and cohesive monostylistic design of cities. These two Chicago architects, Sullivan and Burnham, sparked a debate that would change the face of America.[2]

A century later their conflict of ideals and practices has ascended like a phoenix from the ashes of modernist absolutism. Now, however, an old intellectualism in contemporary guise has arisen to bridge the gap. Here stands the twenty-first-century architect. Here stands the architect eclectic.[3]

Grasping Diderot's notion of eclecticism as a source of motivation, Curtis Worth Fentress and James Henry Bradburn respond: "form follows the poetry of an idea." Alone, function constricts, for the poetry of an idea contains not only the meter of function but the rhythm of site, ecologies, external forces, and human beings. Ultimately, the idea makes things fresh, and the eclectic gives ideas life.

Thus, through the eyes of the architect eclectic, each side of the debate contains the essence of the other. A true synthesis is now born.

Context

In the postmodern era, architects question the appropriateness of any single avant-garde design theory while critics assign a catalogue of names—deconstructivism, poststructuralism, postmodernism—to each design strategy. Yet in the face of this uncertain pastiche, the International Style lives on. For generations architecture has been at the mercy of developing technologies, and modernism's experimentation with new materials and new forms continues.

1. Louis Henri Sullivan, 1900
2. Carson Pirie Scott Building, Chicago, Illinois. Adler and Sullivan, 1906–8

3. Daniel H. Burnham, c. 1882
4. Monadnock Building, Chicago, Illinois. Burnham and Root, 1891

Historicism, categorized under the politically correct yet vague rubric "regionalism" has persisted as an anathema since modernism tried to obliterate it in the years following World War II. A contemporary critic echoes the lament of nineteenth-century scholars: "The lapse into derivative historicism was, then as always, a reflection, in part, of a spiritual and intellectual indolence, a lack of creative vision and courage."[4] Yet historicism's source will continue to determine who will actually win the race to define the stylistic milieu of the last quarter of the twentieth century. Chicago architect John Wellborn Root wrote at the close of the last century:

Architectural styles, national or new, were never discovered by human prospectors however eagerly they have searched. Styles are found truly at the appointed time . . . but solely by those, who, with intelligence and soberness, are working out their ends by the best means at hand, and with scarce a thought of the coming new or national style. Architecture is, like all other art, born of its age and environment. So, the new type will be found by us, if we do find it, through the frankest possible acceptance of every requirement of modern life in all its conditions, without regret for the past or idle longing for a future or more fortunate day.[5]

In our era, the historical paradigm has been overlooked. Such a paradigm demands structuring architectural practice so that it is constantly attuned to the cacophony of international stylistic movements while responding instantly and competently to the needs of a local community. The design path chosen directly responds to the specific situation, the expertise of the firm's design team, and the creativity of the design team's leader and is not restricted to any one stylistic approach. At first glance this may appear as a mere management strategy, and to a limited degree that assumption is correct. This process of problem solving, however, privileges the great thinker, the eclectic who takes an analytical and scientific approach to the task at hand and whose design work resists categorization according to the symbologies of history. This uniquely American path was forged by certain firms following the formation of the American Institute of Architects, which organized the profession in the 1850s. Later modern designers took the same route.[6] It is the path of the true architect eclectic and the route that Fentress Bradburn has chosen.

The Denver International Airport Passenger Terminal Complex is notable in that it is a nonobjective pastiche (fig. 5). Its roof recalls the cable-net experiments of Matthew Nowicki in the 1950s and the tensile-fabric explorations of Frei Otto in the 1960s: a decidedly modern glass enclosure that echoes the intense regularity of the Beaux-Arts (fig. 6). Yet it is new. The former mayor of Denver (now United States transportation secretary), Federico Peña, stated clearly: "We've been searching for a design that would be international in scope and image, that would be unique, like the Sydney Opera House. This is it!"[7] (fig. 7).

The negotiations that led to the design did not consider the tensile-fabric roof constructs of Arthur Erickson's San Diego Convention Center, Downs/Archanbault's Canada Harbour Place in Vancouver, or even Skidmore Owings & Merrill's Haj Terminal in Jeddah, Saudi Arabia, as stylistic precedents but sought a distinct imagery suitable to the surrounding mountains (figs. 8–10).[8] The only "ism" that fits is regionalism, though as previously mentioned, this term is too broad and subsequently not specific enough. In an age that manifests a

5

6

7

8

9

10

5. Denver International Airport
Passenger Terminal Complex,
Denver, Colorado. C.W. Fentress
J.H. Bradburn and Associates, 1994
6. Montreal Experiments. Frei Otto,
1967
7. Sydney Opera House, Sydney,
Australia. Jorn Utzon, 1957–73

8. San Diego Convention Center,
San Diego, California. Arthur
Erickson, 1984
9. Canada Harbor Place, Vancouver,
British Columbia.
Downs/Archanbault, 1986
10. Haj Terminal, Jeddah, Saudi
Arabia. Skidmore Owings &
Merrill, 1981–82

11. *Imperial Hotel, Tokyo, Japan. Frank Lloyd Wright, 1915–22*
12. *Kaufmann House, Bear Run, Pennsylvania. Frank Lloyd Wright, 1936–39*

13. *Glass skyscraper study. Ludwig Mies van der Rohe, 1922*
14. *John Hancock Tower, Boston, Massachusetts. I. M. Pei and Partners, 1973*
15. *Glass House, New Canaan, Connecticut. Philip Johnson, 1956*

polyglot of styles, Fentress Bradburn proposes a new style based upon several older models. This finds expression in a "contextual regionalism" defined by the editor of *Architecture* as "designing for a place."[9]

While critic Charles Jencks has noted the recent development of both contextualism and regionalism, he failed to associate the two in what now best defines this work, which responds not only to human needs but to the existing environment. To Fentress Bradburn, regionalism, within the context of humanism, includes appropriation from the found environment, both urban and natural.[10]

Any stylistic model may serve contextual regionalism, but only if seen through a Wrightian filter. Fundamentally abandoned during the modernist era, this filter dictates that the architect examine the cultural and ecological macrocosm of a place before extrapolating a built microcosm. A new piece of cloth can thus be woven into the architectural fabric of any given place with very little direct historical reference. Examples are Wright's Imperial Hotel in Tokyo and his organic masterpiece, the Kaufmann House in Bear Run, Pennsylvania (figs. 11, 12). Yet Wright fell far short of this when it came to public structures—a building typology key to Fentress Bradburn's success.

During the early years of American architecture, the historical paradigm was influenced first by a French atelier-structured practice. This arrangement, which affected a majority of American firms, addressed the reality that the single architect with a studio full of assistants was frequently too limited to seek and execute work, given the breadth and aggression of the competition as well as the varieties of competitors. Thus developed the pattern of partnerships of at least two principals. One partner was generally concerned with design or philosophical issues and the other with technical or business concerns; the two teamed up to manage the firm. As in Europe, all executed work still bore the names of the partners rather than those of the individuals employed in the studio. The great midwestern firms at the turn of the century, such as Adler and Sullivan, Burnham and Root, Jenney and Mundie, Holabird and Roache, and eastern firms such as Ware and Van Brunt and McKim Mead, and White all took this form. This became the distinctly American model: the firm positioned to address architecture as big business. Daniel H. Burnham, former president of the American Institute of Architects, in an effort to elevate public architecture, added to this structure the drive to involve the government in the business of architecture (not just construction). He further advised: "Make no little plans, they have no magic to stir men's blood."[11] Fentress Bradburn adopted this caveat as a motto. Fentress Bradburn first sought to revive what had been laid to rest by the modernist manifesto and to apply certain Wrightian ideals to large civic commissions, something that Wright himself was not able to accomplish.[12] Fentress and Bradburn also attempted to structure the firm in the tempered American model as a company that could aggressively compete and to "make no little plans."

Both forces were paramount in forming the synthesis that was to become the firm C.W. Fentress J.H. Bradburn and Associates.

Curtis Worth Fentress graduated from North Carolina State University's School of Architecture in 1972 and immediately joined the New York office of celebrated modernist I. M. Pei. There Fentress began to reassess the values of pure modernism and its absolute meaning. He notes the following incident as crucial to his early theoretical experimentation:

During the design development process that brought about the John Hancock Tower in Boston, Pei associate Henry Cobb began to work with a mylar model that in many ways resembled Mies van der Rohe's Design for a Glass Skyscraper of 1922. The model and a drawing of the glass skyscraper became the focal point of an attempt to make a purely glass building. As the design developed, Pei's debt to Mies became increasingly clear. The steel-frame and glass paneled building was as full an expression as possible of Miesien theoretical "minimalist" attempts in the early twenties which would ultimately lead to codified modernism in the thirties. Yet in the late sixties and early seventies developing technologies still hampered the Boston project and caused its near structural, and subsequently legal, disaster.[13] (figs. 13, 14)

According to architect Philip Johnson, a Mies devoté and curator of architecture for the Museum of Modern Art's 1932 exhibition of International Style architecture:[14]

The distinguishing aesthetic principles of the International Style . . . are three: emphasis upon volume—space enclosed by thin planes or surfaces as opposed to the suggestion of mass or solidity; regularity as opposed to symmetry or other kinds of obvious balance; and, lastly, dependence upon the intrinsic elegance of materials, technical perfection, and fine proportions, as opposed to applied ornament.[15]

Johnson's Glass House in New Canaan, Connecticut (1956) attempted to explain the nuances of this modernist manifesto, as had Mies's German Pavilion in Barcelona (1929) and his Farnsworth House in Plano, Illinois (1951) (figs. 15–17). To Fentress, however, the inclusion of the necessary exterior structural details, such as window mullions and/or frames or Mies's decorative I-beams, obstructed any move toward the pure planer geometries advocated by Johnson and the other modernists. Technological limitations had prevented the fullest expressions of modernism, as they continued to do in the John Hancock Tower. Later Pei created in stone what could not be done in glass in his East Wing of the National Gallery in Washington, D. C. (1968–78) (fig. 18).

In 1982, in the footsteps of his mentor Pei, Fentress accomplished one of the first truly glass "modernist" buildings at 116 Inverness Drive East, Englewood, Colorado (frontispiece).[16] Even Norman Foster and Associates' Willis-Faber & Dumas Building in Ipswich, England (1974), Cesar Pelli's Pacific Design Center in West Hollywood, California (1975), and Kohn Pedersen Fox's 333 Wacker Drive in Chicago (1979–83), however stunning, do not compare (figs. 19–21). Fentress's near seamless, banded glass curtain wall, arranged in plan as an X, appears as if carved from ice. Its mirror finish reflecting the rolling plains and mountains of Colorado is a remarkable sight. Moreover, the structure's purity of form proved Johnson's expressed modernist view long after he himself had forsaken it.

Fentress left Pei's office in 1977 to join the newly formed Kohn Pedersen Fox (KPF) to work on a different kind of architecture that advocated a different ethos. Pei had focused on the isolated masterpiece, the individualistic building for the idiosyncratic client, shown best by his work on the Kennedy Library (fig. 22). Commissions for tall, urban-scale structures were infrequent. Fentress had always desired to design big buildings. So did KPF. Thus, the liaison seemed natural.

16

17

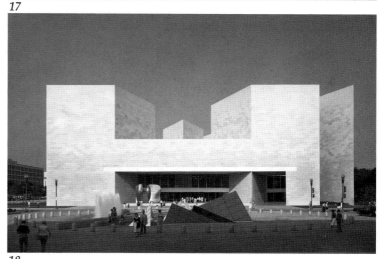

18

16. German Pavilion, Barcelona, Spain. Ludwig Mies van der Rohe, 1929

17. Farnsworth House, Plano, Illinois. Ludwig Mies van der Rohe, 1951

18. East Wing, National Gallery of Art, Washington, D.C. I. M. Pei and Partners, 1968–78

19

20

21

22

19. *Pacific Design Center, West Hollywood, California. Cesar Pelli, 1975*
20. *Willis-Faber & Dumas Building, Ipswich, England. Sir Norman Foster and Partners, Ltd, 1974. Connection detail*

21. *333 Wacker Drive, Chicago, Illinois. Kohn Pedersen Fox, 1983*
22. *John F. Kennedy Library, Boston, Massachusetts. I. M. Pei and Partners, 1964–79*

In 1980, while completing work as the senior designer for KPF's Amoco Building in Denver (1977–80), Fentress decided to launch his own practice based upon business relationships and friendships that he had formed while working in Colorado (fig. 23). Thus, Fentress began his own quest for the American structural model. Introduced by a mutual acquaintance, Fentress and James Henry Bradburn, a 1966 graduate of Rensselaer Polytechnic Institute and formerly of Kevin Roche John Dinkeloo and Associates of Hamden, Connecticut, formed a partnership. Bradburn, a protegé of Dinkeloo, carried with him an exacting knowledge of materiality and production technology, plus a desire to design and construct buildings better than anyone else.

The American paradigm, now evolved through the Roche Dinkeloo pattern, implied that Bradburn would principally address production issues while Fentress focused on design. This model made historical and logical sense to the partners: Bradburn had worked directly with Dinkeloo for twelve years, and Fentress perceived in Roche Dinkeloo a synthesis of the approach developed in Saarinen's office (a practice which he had studied in depth in college). With Fentress's experiences at KPF and I. M. Pei, the two architects had a perfect platform from which to launch a new design practice.

The partnership was an immediate success. The freedom afforded Fentress to explore design aesthetics was paramount, as was Bradburn's ability to pursue his love of construction technologies applied to design. Art and science came together to serve both men. Out of this sprang team participation at the firm rarely matched in drive, enthusiasm, and intensity. Bradburn researched and found a technological solution that served the firm's pursuit of the modernist ideal: the mirrored X of 116 Inverness Drive East has no window framing or external details; an industrial silicone sealant provided the binding catalyst for the glazing, appearing principally within the structure and barely visible without. Fentress had only to apply this to the glass box to achieve a crystalline jewel of a building. Securely tested on this four-story structure, the method soon appeared on the fifty-story Reliance Center (1982) (fig. 24).

Early designs such as One DTC (1985), the Terrace Towers Complex in Englewood, Colorado (1981–86), and 1999 Broadway in Denver (1985) show the influence on the young firm of the partner's past associations with Kohn Pedersen Fox and Roche Dinkeloo, but the technology involved and the articulation of surfaces are distinctly Fentress Bradburn. For example, in the Terrace Towers Complex the visible clear span demanded a more aesthetic treatment than that provided by reinforced concrete or steel. The firm, working with Indiana Limestone, applied a structural post-tensioned spandrel panel that spans the exterior column to column (the first one of this size anywhere). As with the silicone glazing at 116 Inverness Drive East, the limestone panel cautiously tested on the Terrace Towers Complex then rose to forty-five stories on 1999 Broadway (fig. 25).

Fentress Bradburn's design for 1999 Broadway is remarkable in that this office tower shares its urban site with a historic church, each occupying approximately two-thirds of the property. As the firm worked with the church and the developer to reconcile this apparently impossible incongruity, they generated a design acceptable to both while enhancing the urban fabric.

The triangular tower stands on the corner of the lot, the two street facades arranged much like Burnham's Flatiron Building in New York (1901–2), while the remaining faceted facade is raised on freestanding columns and embraces the Holy Ghost Roman Catholic Church. This junction of the two buildings creates a mixture of urban plazas designed to serve the tower occupants during the week and parishioners on the weekend (figs. 26–28).

The final design incorporated a gift to the parish—a masterfully restored church (fig. 29). Fentress Bradburn brought to the Holy Ghost project a polished skill, for the firm had engaged in historic preservation projects for some time. Its first offices, at 16th and Glenarm streets in Denver, were located in the Kittredge Building. Fentress Bradburn restored this 1891 Texas pink granite and rhyolite office block, originally designed by A. Morris Stuckert to be the city's first skyscraper (fig. 30). The firm had also rehabilitated the Navarre, a structure of shady past but great potential, for private art collector Mr. William Foxley in 1983 (fig. 31).[17] The architects along with John Prosser, created within this structure a series of spaces that could be used to display Foxley's collection in a "new" Museum of Western Art.[18] Nonetheless, by 1985 historical preservation had become just one of the firm's many concerns, as they began to engage the issues of public architecture. This necessary refocus and the mastery of preservation skills eventually led to Fentress Bradburn's most significant commission in both fields, however, the restoration and life-safety retrofit of the Colorado State Capitol Building (1989–) (fig. 32).

By now the architects had effectively shed influences from previous design associations. The preservation work undertaken as they launched their practice offered an interesting challenge to a firm whose principal interest was (and continues to be) large public buildings, but it mainly served to regraph the designers' extremely eclectic learning curve. What the architects mastered from concentrated ergonomic examinations of existing interior spaces caused them to reevaluate their entire design impetus. Design for design's sake was not the answer. Historical styles versus modernism was not the issue. The human equation had to be considered. To the architects this rebirth necessitated redefining the philosophical nature of humanism in practical terms of human physical and psychological comfort.

Frank Lloyd Wright, when asked to respond to the tremendous, the tall, the monumental, and the impressive in modern architecture, replied: "The thing in itself is not wrong, but all those buildings were dedicated to the inferiority complex and our declaration of the sovereignty of the individual demands a different sense of proportion . . . . So my scale in the buildings that I built has always been the human scale."[19] For Fentress Bradburn, element one of the Wrightian filter had just fallen into place.

In 1986 New York avant-garde architectural patron Henry Lambert engaged the firm to design a speculative office tower in Tucson, Arizona. This time, instead of approaching the project from the modernist view, Fentress Bradburn measured the opportunity against their concern for humanism. The questions posed addressed both psychological comfort and local inhabitants' recollections of home. Wide, spacious plazas with raised planters for seating and springlike water features of the desert oasis appeared in the plans (fig. 33).

23

26

24

27

25

28

23. *Amoco Building, Denver, Colorado. Kohn Pedersen Fox, 1980*
24. *Reliance Tower, Denver, Colorado. C.W. Fentress and Associates, 1982*
25. *1999 Broadway, Denver, Colorado. C.W. Fentress and Associates, 1985. 18th Street facade*

26. *Flatiron Building, New York, New York. D. H. Burnham and Company, 1903*
27. *1999 Broadway, Denver, Colorado. C.W. Fentress and Associates, 1985*
28. *1999 Broadway, Denver, Colorado. C.W. Fentress and Associates, 1985*

29

32

30

33

31

34

29. Holy Ghost Roman Catholic
Church, Denver, Colorado. Restored
by C.W. Fentress and Associates,
1985
30. Kittredge Building, Denver,
Colorado. A. Morris Stuckert, 1881
31. The Navarre, Denver, Colorado.
Frank E. Edbrooke, 1880

32. Colorado State Capitol, Denver,
Colorado. Elijah E. Meyers, 1894
33. United Bank Plaza, Tucson,
Arizona. C.W. Fentress and
Associates, 1986
34. United Bank Tower, Tucson,
Arizona. C.W. Fentress and
Associates, 1986

The architects also studied the archives of ancient and modern southwestern built form and finally focused on the Spanish church (fig. 34). This building type was centrally urban, and its steeples rising above the cactus evoked a powerful cultural memory. The historical imagery of the southwest had never, however, been applied to the skin of a skyscraper.

The resulting structure bears a certain coincidental similarity to the Procter and Gamble Headquarters in Cincinnati (1982–85) by Kohn Pedersen Fox, but Fentress Bradburn's motivation was clearly different (fig. 35). KPF acknowledged the influence of art deco seen in Wright's Unity Temple (1909), while Fentress Bradburn recalled the Spanish church (figs. 36, 37).[20] That the two complexes were similar in style even though approached from divergent viewpoints concerned the architects a great deal.

It was becoming evident that the search for an obvious postmodern image had led to a broad, semihistorical neoclassicism that evoked not the lofty imagery espoused by recognized firms such as KPF and emerging ones such as Fentress Bradburn but a classicism popular during the 1930s and early forties, unkindly called "FDR post-office moderne" but properly labeled by Jencks as a version of stripped classicism. The recognition of this uncomfortable trend, which had led to the stylistic overlap of this instance, motivated Fentress Bradburn to revisit the idea of evoked cultural memory. The firm concluded that it is not enough to seek imagery in built form alone: the true meaning of Wright's "organic" architectural principles was becoming clear.

Fentress Bradburn began at once to stress the premise that the place upon which one imposes a structure is, above all, the sum of its parts. It was to all of the parts that the firm now turned. Issues such as general landscape, specific topography, and ecology took on increasing importance, not because they had to be mapped to build successfully but because of the imagery that they evoked, the additional cultural memory stimulated in the inhabitants, and the organic individuality of each site's fabric. Future projects would include analyses of native costume, flora and fauna, and land form and coloration. The historicism that played the premier role in the development of the United Bank Tower in Tucson would no longer be a major factor. Wright himself had stated that "organic architecture . . . is the architecture of nature . . . the architecture based upon principle and not upon precedent." The second element of the Wrightian filter was now in place. The germ of an idea now sprouted a well-defined design tree. The branches of this new standard found expression in humanist terms, in the philosophy that form follows the poetry of an idea that stresses the importance of context. These were the essential fibers of the filter. It was left to the architects to make that filter work.

Neither culture nor ecology is static. The challenge for the designer is to grasp the right pieces of thread at precisely the right moment to provide the necessary weave for his new bolt of architectural cloth.

As both elements are mutable, it can be extremely difficult to make a project cohere. The architect must remain alert to any and all possibilities. A common problem associated with animate culture is fluctuations in associated economies—both local and project specific. Failure in either area may cause a project to collapse. As for animate ecology, relying too heavily on the precedent of a previously built environment may mean repeating past mistakes. Fentress Bradburn's design for the Colorado Convention Center (1990) addressed these dilemmas and paved the way for the firm's focus on public architecture in the 1990s.

The 1989 rehabilitation of the Denver Permit Center had afforded the architects the opportunity to meet and work with many of the politicians and bureaucrats who would be involved in future projects in the Denver metropolitan area (fig. 38). It also taught them how to design to the determinations of a committee and reintroduced them to a historical player in the realm of public building: the artist. The challenge of the one-percent-for-art program, which was introduced to the architects as part of the public building process, presented an opportunity to reinvestigate lighting technique and display quality, which had been previously addressed in the firm's museum projects. Fentress Bradburn also realized that to succeed in the public arena, the firm needed to consider the artist as integral to the design process.[21] Work by graphic artists and sculptors appeared in subsequent projects.

Fentress Bradburn emerged as the unlikely winner of the 1990 Colorado Convention Center competition because several serious extraneous factors influenced the selection process. Myriad political entanglements drove the competition.

Initially the mayor of Denver had pressed for a site in lower downtown near Union Station, but the voters rejected any placement in that vicinity. Recognizing the mayor's reluctance to pursue a new center after this defeat, the architectural community, led by Fentress Bradburn, continued to champion the idea. Thus, the architects as promoters began to search for a more appropriate site. Fentress Bradburn elaborated a proposal to expand the older Currigan Exhibition Hall convention complex without requiring the purchase of additional land. As the firm pressed forward with its design, the architects met continuing resistance. Finally, in a private meeting, one of Denver's city councilmen told the firm that the issue had indeed been placed back on the City's agenda, that a competition had been held, and that a site had been chosen. The rather shocking news not only concerned the firm, it evoked the ire of several powerful landowners as well. It was clear that some back-room dealing had been done, which the local press leaped to expose.

The resultant political scuffle brought two additional sites to the fore as candidates. Now there were three: the secret winner of the supposed competition, referred to as the Golden Triangle and presented by developer Al Cohen, the Currigan Hall site chosen by Fentress Bradburn with developer David French, and a third site along the Platte River belonging to billionaire developer Philip Anschutz.

In a political maneuver apparently to secure the Platte River site, Anschutz lobbied the Colorado State Legislature to help the City acquire the land. The legislature responded that it would budget 36 million dollars to help, but only if it had oversight of the property selection process through the Urban Land Institute—dictating true and open competition for both site and adaptive design.

Fentress Bradburn, strengthened by their own design convictions and the belief that they had the best siting

35

36

37

38

35. Proctor & Gamble Headquarters, Cincinnati, Ohio. Kohn Pedersen Fox, 1982–85
36. Cincinnati Times Star Building, Cincinnati, Ohio. Samuel Hannaford and Sons, 1931

37. Unity Temple, Oak Park, Illinois. Frank Lloyd Wright, 1906. Interior
38. Denver Permit Center, Denver, Colorado. C.W. Fentress and Associates, 1989

39

40

41

42

43

44

39. *Colorado Convention Center, Denver, Colorado. C.W. Fentress J.H. Bradburn and Associates, 1990*
40. *Colorado Convention Center, Denver, Colorado. C.W. Fentress J.H. Bradburn and Associates, 1990*
41. *Colorado Convention Center, Denver, Colorado. C.W. Fentress J.H. Bradburn and Associates, 1990*

42. *Erick Johnson,* Tail Spin, *1990*
43. *Steve Devries,* Prismatic Installation, *1990*
44. *Barbara Jo Revelle,* Colorado Panorama: A People's History, *1990*

solution, entered the contest knowing that they had only an outside chance to win because the City still favored Cohen's Golden Triangle site. The competition, which included the well-funded developers and architects secured by Cohen, Thompson, Ventulett, Stainback and Associates of Atlanta, and Anschutz's entry by I. M. Pei, appeared an overwhelming hurdle to the small partnership. Fentress Bradburn's entry, however, which in the interim had been developed considerably beyond predesign, was presented so well that the selection committee accepted it unanimously as the winner. One local newspaper recorded Denver city officials as being "stunned" at the choice.[22] Fortunately for the participants, the surprise was not directed at them but at the fact that the Golden Triangle location had not been chosen and that the big names and large funding had been passed over.

The final site, adjacent to Currigan Exhibition Hall, is delineated by Speer Boulevard and 14th Street, and Stout and Welton streets. *Denver Business Magazine* stated: "Before it was built, critics complained about the center's location; now most businesses say the center ended up right where most people thought it should have been in the first place—in the heart of downtown Denver."[23] Fentress describes the force driving the firm's choice in siting and design:

Our situation was that of the American architect Raymond Hood before he won the Chicago Tribune Tower competition: we were very near to closing our doors. As had Hood, we won the competition based on our ideas, wisdom, and tenacity of belief. Sometimes a competition can bring out the best in an architect. Sometimes a competition can start a career on a new path. In this case it did. Our team recognized the importance of the contest for those with the courage to persist. In the face of that, we stood firm in our convictions and were fortunate to prevail.[24]

While the Denver Permit Building commission had introduced the firm to working with politicians, the Colorado Convention Center competition introduced them to politics and issues and stirred a renewed sense of purpose.

The project's master plan called for two building phases, one on this site and the second to replace Currigan Hall. The 14th Street facade was set back to align with the front of the hall, so that plazas for the two buildings would flow as a continuous open space. The design of the main downtown entrance's northeast facade on 14th at California Street was virtually repeated on the opposite side. Both entries have broad panoramic views. The downtown entry, whose view is of the Denver cityscape, is concave, offering outstretched arms in a welcoming gesture to pedestrians (a theme to be repeated in subsequent Fentress Bradburn projects). The southwestern entry is convex, functioning as a three-story bay window from which conventioneers can view the Rocky Mountains (figs. 39–41).[25]

Two of three entrances feature sculptures specifically designed for the space. The design team invested long hours working with sculptors Erick Johnson and Steve Devries to achieve the proper balance of lighting to object and object to architectural space (figs. 42–44). Barbara Jo Revelle created a tile mural from a digitized photograph for the third (utility) entrance.

By gently opening spaces in the urban fabric and addressing the street-level pedestrian, the firm created an art of grid

45

46

47

45. *Colorado Convention Center, Denver, Colorado. C.W. Fentress J.H. Bradburn and Associates, 1990*

46. *Thomas Jefferson Memorial, Washington, D.C. John Russell Pope, 1937*

47. *Jefferson County Government Center Courts and Administration Building, Golden, Colorado. C.W. Fentress J.H. Bradburn and Associates, 1993. Dome detail*

density without urban-canyon mentality, thus averting a common building mistake in Denver and other typically American versions of the village aping the metropolis. Consequently, the center, which has drawn small businesses and hotels to its proximity, has revitalized a needy portion of the city.

The imagery of mountain forests and geological strata of the nearby hills finds a built synthesis in this very urban structure, completing a twofold humanist and organic attack (fig. 45).[26]

With the introduction of this large public commission into the firm's repertoire and with the new skills acquired in dealing with government bodies, Fentress Bradburn acknowledged a renewed sense of purpose, making a deliberate transition to the architecture of democracy. Their great mentor Wright further inspired this shift: "There must be coming from us—to us—something out of democracy in the way of a freedom which has its basis in nature. The study of nature not the study of anything or any system or any synthetic system of knowledge ever promulgated. It must be original."[27]

While Frank Lloyd Wright would have admired portions of Fentress Bradburn's next series of public projects, he may not have praised larger portions of the Jefferson County Government Center in Golden, Colorado. Wright had elaborated his aversion to domed civic centers in his Kahn Lectures at Princeton in 1930:

From general to particular the imitation proceeds, from the dome of the National Capitol itself to the dome of the State Capitol. From the State Capitol to the dome of the County Court House on down to the dome of the City Hall. Everywhere the symbol leaves us, for our authority, in debt to Michelangelo for life . . . . But the tyrannical dome is a magniloquent waste. How tragic it all is!

Domed or damned was and is the status of official buildings in all countries, especially in ours, as a consequence of the great Italian's impulsive indiscretion.[28]

Fentress Bradburn was aware of the need for a new synthesis of imagery for this county courthouse, but the county commissioners were not completely sensitive to it. They wished, at least in concept, for an echo of John Russell Pope's Jefferson Memorial in Washington, D.C. (figs. 46, 47). The resulting design featured a centrally domed rotunda. However, the architects made the rotunda transparent and reduced the radius of its arc to that of Pope's to lessen its severity.

The completed 125-foot-high central rotunda functions as a hinge to secure two radial sets of arms that comprise the building's office blocks. These arcs form a welcoming gesture, presenting to citizens the appearance of an open and accessible government. As a lantern on the landscape, the rotunda also serves as a beacon to the county center in the evening and begins to define a series of courtyards both interior and exterior, public and private, that humanize the mass while serving the needs of electorate and county employee alike.

The atrium's expanse of glazing addresses a significant factor of the firm's burgeoning investigation into sustainable architecture. As at the Colorado Convention Center, daylight

here visually integrates the outdoors and indoors while reducing lighting costs. The isolation of the rotunda fenestration from the building wings conserves a significant amount of heating energy as well.

Public corridors extending from this atrium into the wings provide building orientation and expansive views of the countryside and the adjacent open space that was part of the master plan. Elevator lobbies on every floor provide panoramas of the lobby rotunda and complete the visual continuity of the public circulation path.

Externally, these circulation paths are differentiated in massing, window size and transparency, and building skin color. The building's publicly accessible areas are lighter in shade than the sections occupied by the staff. The building's primary inspiration for the coloration and detailing on both exterior and interior derives from the natural mineral and plant forms found on the hilltop on which the building stands.

The finished building is said to inspire a return to the historical center of regional life, the county courthouse. That it stands at all is a monument to the firm's perseverance in getting the job done even in the face of political intrigue. The opposition, questioning the need for a new structure, reintroduced the debate in the public forum and succeeded in turning the electorate against the project, then under construction. The incumbent commissioners, alarmed at unrest stirring within their constituent ranks, attempted to focus on the structure's private funding arrangement. Nonetheless, the contrived groundswell of popular distaste for the project promptly swept most of the commissioners out of office. The incoming opposition completed the building on schedule and within budget.

In 1991 the design received a Citation for Excellence in Architecture for Justice from the American Institute of Architects.

Setting the stage for success in the 1990s and beyond is the firm's Natural Resources Building in Olympia, Washington (1992). This design captured the jurors of the second national competition that Fentress Bradburn entered. Winning this contest outside of the firm's own metroplex and against larger, nationally recognized firms bolstered the architects' confidence. Recent victories in national and international competitions have secured commissions for Las Vegas's Clark County Government Center and the New Seoul International Airport in South Korea.

Fentress Bradburn translates the metaphor of microcosm and macrocosm, so fundamental to humanist thought, into a new language. In the firm's projects, the anthropomorphic and anthropometric relationship of man to architecture remains intimate, subtle, implied. The relationship of architecture to the environment derives from the region, generating a contextual regionalism.

Projects now on the boards reveal mature work delicately sensible to the tasks and purposes set forth in this volume, produced by a fully emerged synthesis of mind among Curtis Fentress, James Bradburn, and the team of inspired young designers that they have assembled.

"Form follows the poetry of an idea" now also embraces the desires of the entire assembled cast, which declares its intent in a collective vision. This corporate mind operates as that of a great thinker on the verge of a new discovery.

Architectural historian Thomas Hines describes the phenomenon of such architectural eclectics: "The Sullivans, Burnhams, and Wrights of our history have been distinct and different voices, separate and unmergeable. As students of history, we accept that and continue trying to understand them all—while knowing, here and now, that as citizens and architects, there is always the need and possibility of synthesis."[29]

This premise is continually pressed to the fore by the creative and individualistic patterns of late twentieth-century architecture. To this list we must add the designs of C.W. Fentress J.H. Bradburn and Associates. For this work reveals clearly the exciting possibilities brought about by a true synthesis of mind expressed in the lyric poetry of an architectural idea.

Notes
1. Charles Jencks, *Architecture Today* (New York: Harry N. Abrams, 1988), 270.
2. Thomas S. Hines, *Burnham of Chicago: Architect and Planner* (New York: Oxford University Press, 1974), 44, 49, and 64.
3. "An eclectic is a philosopher who tramples underfoot prejudice, tradition, seniority, universal consent, authority, and everything which subjugates mass opinion; who dares to think for himself, go back to the clearest general principles, examine them, discuss them, and accept nothing except on the evidence of his own experience and reason; and who, from all the philosophies which he has analyzed without respect to persons, and without partiality, makes a philosophy of his own, peculiar to himself." Diderot, as quoted in Peter Collins, *Changing Ideals in Modern Architecture* (Montreal: McGill-Queens University Press, 1965), 17.
4. Hines, *Burnham,* 368.
5. Ibid., 27.
6. One of the best examples of the evolution of such an approach can be seen in the firm of Eero Saarinen as it became Kevin Roche John Dinkeloo and Associates of Hamden, Connecticut.
7. *Construction News* (New York: McGraw Hill), February 17, 1993, 1.
8. The secondary issue of engineering was addressed after the diverse requirements of place had been satisfied.
9. Deborah Dietsch, editor-in-chief, *Architecture,* personal conversation, 1994.
10. Curtis W. Fentress as quoted in "Learning from Las Vegas? The Clark County Government Center," *Competitions* 2 (Winter 1992): 35.
11. Hines, *Burnham,* xvii.
12. Henry-Russell Hitchcock and Philip Johnson, *The International Style* (New York: W. W. Norton and Company, 1932) became the modernist manifesto by which International Style architecture was measured from 1932 on.
13. Curtis W. Fentress, personal conversation, 1994.
14. Ibid.
15. As summarized in the preface by Alfred Barr in Hitchcock and Johnson, *The International Style,* 13.
16. It can be argued, and quite rightly, that the precedent set by Mies van der Rohe's German Pavilion in Barcelona, Le Corbusier's Villa Savoye, or Howe and Lescaze's Pennsylvania Savings Fund Society Building in Philadelphia truly instigated the International Style. But the International Style passed into modernism, and the tenets of such, set down by Hitchcock and Johnson, were constantly tried and found wanting because of the limitations of technology. This is how such a small work achieved a first in modernism.
    According to Dow Chemical's inventory, the first four-sided, structurally glazed silicone building was the Kaufmann Department Store in Mifflin, Pennsylvania. It was completed in 1980 while 116 Inverness Drive East was still in design, but 116 Inverness Drive East was the first monolithic structure made of insulated glass.
17. Built in 1880, this building had served as a hotel, a school for girls, a casino, a jazz club, a restaurant, and a brothel.
18. Fentress was asked to articulate the basis for his alterations to the Navarre. His reply, "Preservation Requires Skill" (*Rocky Mountain News,* 284 [Denver: Scripps-Howard], January 31, 1984, B29), appeared shortly after the Museum of Western Art opened to the public.
This was not the last time the designer was called upon to address the nature of his work, but it did explain the team's detailed examination of past and future building programs, which led to subtleties such as consciously air-conditioning the people and not the art—a difficult task in a fixed building shell—while not altering the structure's historic character.
19. From a conversation with Dr. Lyman Bryson on December 29, 1958, as recorded in *The Master Architect: Conversations with Frank Lloyd Wright,* ed. Patrick J. Meehan, AIA (New York: John Wiley & Sons, 1984), 73.
20. *Kohn Pedersen Fox: Buildings and Projects 1976–1986,* ed. Trevor D. Abramson and Sonia R. Cháo (New York: Rizzoli International, 1987), 88, 94.
21. The Denver Permit Center had been redesigned around the notion of user-friendly space, which included the visual comfort of works conceived specifically for the architecture and vice versa. In fact, the entry tower was designed to include artwork within the volume. The architect's final design was correlated with that of the sculptor, Erick Johnson, specifically to encapsulate and complement his work.
22. *Rocky Mountain News,* 129 (Denver: Scripps-Howard), August 29, 1987, A1.
23. Glen Richardson, "Meetings Come to Order," *Denver Business* 12, no. 10 (June 1990): 21.
24. Curtis W. Fentress, personal conversation, 1994.
25. Richardson, "Meetings Come to Order," 22, 23.
26. For further possible stylistic influence see: Abramson and Cháo, eds., *Kohn Pederson Fox,* 64–69.
27. Meehan, *The Master Architect,* 187.
28. Frank Lloyd Wright, *Modern Architecture: Being the Kahn Lectures for 1930* (Carbondale, Ill.: Southern Illinois University Press, 1987), 83–84.
29. Hines, *Burnham,* 369.

CHAPTER TWO

Contextual Regionalism in Place

Frontispiece. Denver International Airport Passenger Terminal Complex, Denver, Colorado. C.W. Fentress J.H. Bradburn and Associates, 1994. Mast detail

Above. Colorado landscape

We have, as the Egyptians had or the Chinese, as the Greeks and our own ancestors in the Middle Ages before us, a style which orders the visible manifestation of a certain close relationship between structure and function. Regardless of specific types of structure or of function, the style has a definable aesthetic. That aesthetic, like modern technics, will develop and change; it will hardly cease to exist. It is found in the humblest buildings, as well as in monuments, fully architectural. Those who have buried architecture, whether from a thwarted desire to continue the past or from an over-anxiety to modify and hurry on the future, have been premature: We have an architecture still.—Henry-Russell Hitchcock[1]

The design of the Denver International Airport's new Passenger Terminal Complex is not given to subtleties. Spatially massive, it also presses the limits of experimental technology. The structure extends the range of aesthetic applications of certain materials; its state-of-the-art technology required that the contractors develop new systems to accommodate the design. Glass curtain walls cantilever off the floor and gossamer peaks form a roof in a part of eastern Colorado that has been known to register wind gusts of over one hundred miles per hour and several feet of snowfall in a few hours. In short, it is a breathtaking work of art. C.W. Fentress J.H. Bradburn and Associates' team of design specialists literally calculated every square inch of the project. They tested the cable-net stresses of the tensile-fabric roof in the laboratory and *in situ*. They made multiple fact-finding trips to other fabric structures, catalogued their advantages and disadvantages, and factored each into the design calculations. Denver International Airport boasts the largest structurally integrated, tensile-membrane roof in the world. (The larger fabric roof of Skidmore Owings & Merrill's Haj Terminal in Jeddah, Saudi Arabia, does not structurally enclose the space; it only serves as a canopy.) Fentress Bradburn pushed the limits of available technology of a structural design system explored first in the 1950s as cable net and expressed most graphically in the 1960s as its evolutionary extension, tensile membrane.

The research begun in the fifties by American architects such as Matthew Nowicki and William Henry Deitrick and engineers such as Fred N. Severud prompted German architect Frei Otto and others to experiment with such systems in the following decade. Otto claimed that Nowicki's designs for the Raleigh, North Carolina, Dorton Arena initiated his quest for useful cable-net and tensile-membrane designs (fig. 1). A series of studies at Raleigh's North Carolina State College School of Design by international architects and theorists, including Horacio Caminos of Spain, Felix Candela of Mexico, Eduardo Catalano of Argentina, and others following in the footsteps of the great art nouveau master, Antonio Gaudi, placed this school in the investigative forefront of expressionist structural typologies (figs. 2, 3).[2] For Fentress Bradburn, this connection extends even further, from Severud's technically developmental work through his association with Eero Saarinen at Dulles International Airport in Washington, D.C., the TWA terminal at New York's John F. Kennedy International Airport, and the Jefferson Memorial Arch in Saint Louis, masterpieces of Saarinen's career (figs. 4–6). This legacy presented the architects with the opportunity to extend personal research into a concentrated team approach. Bradburn brought his background in working with experimental systems under John Dinkeloo, formerly head of production in Saarinen's office. Fentress brought his personal connection with the early cable-net experiments at North Carolina State College and a wealth of firsthand experience with Nowicki's Raleigh Arena and the theoretical

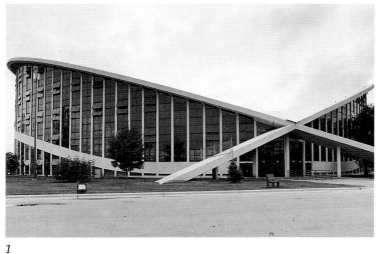

1

2

3

4

examinations of structural systems that had garnered worldwide fame for Fentress's alma mater.[3] Fentress's affection for Saarinen's designs had also led to an intimate understanding of the work's materiality and expression and the young man's subliminal desire to pattern his own career after Saarinen's. Nevertheless, the opportunity to reexamine these historic treatises or even to design in the Saarinen mold did not present itself to the architects until the Denver International Airport project.

To Fentress's additional advantage, his thesis had concerned airports. From this he had concluded that no major airports were likely to be built during his architectural career. Cataloguing this as a bit of professional bad fortune, Fentress had dismissed the notion of designing an airport long before the Denver International project was announced. Suddenly the opportunity arose, and his team of architects was positioned better than ever to execute such a commission. An added incentive was the chance to design the passenger terminal complex for the world's largest airport.

After requesting that a limited number of firms submit their qualifications, the City appeared to have dealt the airport job to Perez Architects of New Orleans, whom it had already employed at Stapleton International Airport. The initial architect's participation, however, was limited to developing design standards, 30 percent of the total contract. This would tap a skill acquired at the older airport. Perez could also submit a design based upon those standards, but the selection of the architect-of-record and final design team would occur later. Early reviews of the designs and drawings developed by the original firm raised questions about price, constructibility, and construction schedule. Moreover, Denver mayor Federico Peña was not happy with the concept, labeling it "not memorable." The construction management firm Lehrer McGovern Bovis of New York, employed to review the work to date, estimated a budgetary overrun of approximately 78 million dollars and reported that the estimated schedule was thirty-eight to forty months too long. This professional opinion reinforced the decision to change course and redesign.

Fentress Bradburn's initial contribution to the terminal project was a design review of the project to date. The result of this investigation confirmed the City's previously commissioned studies. Upon review of the data, William E. Smith, associate director of aviation for the new airport, summoned the principals to his office. He first reminded them that responsibility for complying with budget and schedule would rest with the architect-of-record. Then noting that the comprehensive design concept as depicted in the master plan was not to be altered, he unexpectedly gave the architects three weeks to investigate ways to alleviate the schedule and budget problems. In addition they were to develop a new aesthetic to satisfy the mayor's desire for a "memorable" building reflective of Denver and Colorado. With this charge the architects began an intense charrette, completely redesigning the terminal without altering the comprehensive airport design concept. They reevaluated the entire building's structure to reduce cost and enhance flexibility. The result was a completely new aesthetic.

Fentress Bradburn's contextual regionalism suggested that an evocation of Rocky Mountain imagery would produce a significant form. Specifically, they looked west from the site to the undulating, snow-capped peaks of the Continental Divide piercing the vast blue Colorado sky. How were the designers to capture the essence of this natural metaphor in architecture? The answer was to build so as not to restrict the sky and design to complement the earth.

Fentress brought to the discussion the cable-net systems of Saarinen's airport architecture and other expressionist roof designs spawned by it, such as that of Jørn Utzon's Sydney Opera (1957–73). Fentress's original sketches and models recall the folded plate, or folded paper, designs of such predecessors (fig. 7). Bradburn suggested fabric and cable.

Within a week the architects had begun the information-gathering process for such a technologically oriented solution. While Bradburn visited existing tensile-fabric structures, the rest of the design team made models, assimilating his investigation by telephone. In three weeks the firm presented the completely synthesized design to the City's airport engineer and the airport manager.

The canopy of translucent, Teflon-coated fabric met with much skepticism. Sketches and photographs facilitated further dialogue, as the models did not help to sell the new design. Questions about its ability to withstand Denver's climate led the discussions, but the architects and consulting engineers' assurances turned the talk away from the technical issues of longevity to constructibility and finally to the imagery provided by the new roof system. Encouraged by the gradual acceptance of their ideas, the architects eased through the interview with the Blue Ribbon [Selection] Committee to gain unanimous approval. Despite the government's reluctance to begin the design process afresh, Mayor Peña's demand for a memorable design drove deeper and deeper into the debate. Finally, the City agreed to the new design.

With the major aesthetic design issues resolved, Fentress Bradburn turned to the specific questions of timeliness of construction, budgetary oversight, and longevity and constructibility of the proposed terminal. As the architects produced construction documents, design teams examined aesthetic and technological details. Multiple drawings and models offered views and sections. Specific issues such as daylighting, curbside loading and unloading, and interior transportation connections, as well as finish details, were explored. A fast-track system ensured that individual sections and components were completed while others were being designed.

As the project progressed, the City repeatedly delayed the facility's opening. Nonetheless, the ultimate winners appear to be the citizens of Denver, for the realization of this central transportation hub has already generated an increase in the number of companies willing to consider relocating or establishing branches in Colorado.

Experientially, Denver International Airport is exciting.[4] As one approaches its fifty-three-square-mile site, one confronts the jagged peaks of the passenger terminal's one-thousand-foot-long roof. The new facility visually expresses the desire of the city fathers to create a world hub exploiting Denver's geographic location (an equilateral triangle centered around the North Pole, with sides of approximately four thousand miles, connects Denver to Tokyo and Frankfurt).

5

6

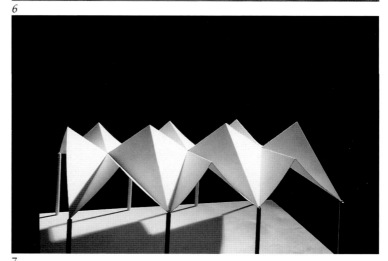

7

1. J. S. Dorton Arena, Raleigh, North Carolina. Matthew Nowicki, 1951
2. Catenary Study. Eduardo Catalano, 1960
3. School of the Sagrada Familia, Barcelona, Spain. Antonio Gaudi, 1909. Roof detail
4. Dulles International Airport, Chantilly, Virginia. Eero Saarinen, 1958–62

5. TWA Terminal, John F. Kennedy International Airport, New York, New York. Eero Saarinen, 1960
6. Jefferson Memorial Arch, Saint Louis, Missouri. Eero Saarinen, 1953–56
7. Denver International Airport Passenger Terminal Complex, Denver, Colorado. Curtis Worth Fentress, 1992. Preliminary roof design

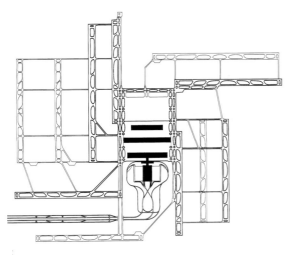

8

9

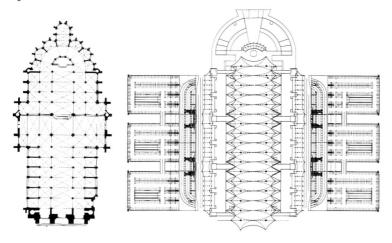

10   11

8. *Runway Design, Denver International Airport, Denver, Colorado, 1992*

9. *Denver International Airport Passenger Terminal Complex, Denver, Colorado. C.W. Fentress J.H. Bradburn and Associates, 1994. Curbside canopy*

10. *Cathedral, Amiens, France, 1220–70. Plan*

11. *Denver International Airport Passenger Terminal Complex, Denver, Colorado. C.W. Fentress J.H. Bradburn and Associates, 1994. Plan*

The new airport's parti resembles that of the Smith and Wilkenson's Hartsfield-Atlanta Airport (1980). It is both logical and relatively simple for the traveler to comprehend. As at Atlanta, an invisible spine formed by an underground rail line connects the passenger terminal at the south end to the row of concourses straddling it to the north. Runways form a pinwheel pattern parallel to the spine to the north and south and perpendicular to it to the east and west (fig. 8). Every component of the facility can easily expand without interrupting the airport's functioning.

Canopies stretching the full length of the two upper-level curbsides are the first visible tensile structural elements, announcing the architecture to arriving travelers in an almost subliminal transition from outdoors to indoors (fig. 9). Travelers entering the passenger terminal complex through this porte cochere find themselves in a space flooded with natural light from the translucent fabric ceiling overhead and the glass walls around.

Adopting the principles of the medieval cathedral, two rows of columns, spaced 150 feet apart, extend down the nine-hundred-foot-long great hall, creating a nave, with each row supporting a row of seventeen peaked roof cells (figs. 10, 11). Spanning a width of 210 feet between the clerestory walls, the roof cells enclose a space almost three times the size of the Grand Central Station terminal in New York City.

While Fentress Bradburn shares with the cathedral builders of the past the spirit of turning construction technology into art, everything else about this structure points to an architectural future as advanced as the planes it serves. The result is a space of great simplicity, clarity, and visual diversity.

Triangular clerestory windows on the east and west sides and huge glass endwalls on the south and north are supported by cable trusses, blending with the tensile character of the space and revealing the generous roof overhangs and their sweeping edge catenaries on the outside.

The project exploits four types of cable applications. Unlike early nineteenth-century cable experiments such as Washington and John Roebling's Brooklyn Bridge, where cables simply provide linear support, tensile-membrane structures, subject to most of the same forces, demand cabling in multiple directions (figs. 12, 13). In the terminal, ridge cables, draped over two masts and restrained by anchors on the rigid roof outside, are spaced sixty feet apart. Their shape resembles that of the main cables in a Roebling bridge, enabling them to carry the downward snow loads. Valley cables, shaped like arches and located between ridge cables, resist upward forces, predominantly those caused by wind flowing over the building. Edge catenaries, scalloping into the roof membrane's surface, form the roof's perimeter and are visible through windows all around the building. The membrane shape created by a continuous fabric stress pattern and stretched between these ridge, valley, and edge cables gives the roof its geological form. Finally, radial cables running diagonally from the mast tops to the exterior anchor points help control wind stresses and provide additional restraints.

Most of the vertical masts rise 104 feet above the main floor of the great hall. Two groups of four shafts, located on the borders between the three terminals, are 125 feet high. They articulate the main entrances, add variety to the peaked forms, and give the building a distinct character. (fig. 14, frontispiece).

The canopy, with a total surface area of 377,000 square feet, is continuous over the full length of the passenger terminal and requires no expansion joints because of the flexibility of the folded fabric shape and its tensile members. On each end, a full module forms a canopy suspended from an array of masts and anchor cables. The cable anchor system on the rigid roofs on the long sides of the terminal building contains "octopus" connectors, located at the bottom ends of the valley cables and forming the intersection point of numerous cables. The roof's prestress was introduced by jacking these connectors downward along vertical tie-down cables. Thus, the passenger terminal's canopy becomes the critical visual element in defining interior space and exterior massing. Form and structure are one; art and science, inseparable.

Such integrated design is not easily accomplished within the conventional organization of architectural design teams. It requires architects who are exceptionally receptive to the use and expression of technology and who have the capacity to use technology as a tool in the design process. Fentress Bradburn carries this synthesis into all of their designs.

While Dr. Dwayne Nuzum, dean of the University of Colorado's New College of Architecture and Planning, speculates that this airport will "equal the strength of the designs of Eero Saarinen at Dulles and John F. Kennedy,"[5] the firm's consulting engineer brings a more personal euphoria to his analysis of the roof design.

The results are . . . visible: an interior space of formal dignity, calm, and grace, lightened by the joyous curvatures of the roof membrane and abundant daylight, will greet travelers arriving in Denver. On the outside, the peaks and valleys will not simply resemble the nearby snowy mountains but will remind us of the semi-nomadic nature of our contemporary society and its historic links to . . . the native Americans who once inhabited the area. Not unlike . . . early tent structures, the building will be respectful of the natural environment, reduce energy waste and pollution, bring in light, reflect heat, and relate visually to the world around it. And during the night, the structure will glow gently, visible from the arriving planes and from the nearby city of Denver.[6]

Unenlightened critics often question innovative strategies or point to past failures. To antagonists of innovation Charles Jencks offers the following caveat: "If conflict is built into a democratic architecture then it should be supported by a dual criticism, which acknowledges the ambiguity that is an integral part of architectural experience. Any good, complex building elicits a 'yes/but' response and the 'but' is essential to our granting, even understanding the 'yes.'"[7] For Fentress Bradburn, a poetic synthesis of art and science contains the answer to the quintessential "but" that ultimately gives rise to the full understanding of the "yes."

Notes
1. Henry-Russell Hitchcock and Philip Johnson, *The International Style* (New York: W. W. Norton and Company, 1932), 95.
2. The school had on its list of patrons and subscribers to its literary journals Buckminster Fuller and Philip Johnson.
3. See *Student Publications of the School of Design* (Raleigh: North Carolina State College) 5, no. 3 (1956); 6, no. 1 (1956); 6, no. 3 (1957); 9, no. 2 (1960); 10, no. 1 (1960).
4. Consulting engineer Horst Berger details some of the following in "Modern Basilica," *Fabrics & Architecture* (May–June 1993): 10–21.
5. Dean Dwayne Nuzum's comments are recorded in "How will DIA Fly?" *Colorado Business* (August 1993): 52–54.
6. Berger, "Modern Basilica," 21.
7. Charles Jencks, *Architecture Today* (New York: Harry N. Abrams, 1988), 270.

12

13

14

12. *Brooklyn Bridge, Brooklyn, New York. John and Washington Roebling, 1869–83*
13. *Denver International Airport Passenger Terminal Complex, Denver, Colorado. C.W. Fentress J.H. Bradburn and Associates, 1994. Catenary scallop*
14. *Denver International Airport Passenger Terminal Complex, Denver, Colorado. C.W. Fentress J.H. Bradburn and Associates, 1994. Mast detail*

SELECTED WORKS

Major Projects

This multifaceted project deals first with the requirements of place and second with the designers' need to explore new technologies.

The guiding motive for 116 Inverness Drive East, located on rolling hills just east of the Rocky Mountain foothills, was to preserve mountain views and minimize the impact of buildings on the site.

Located at the main entrance to an 840-acre park, the building sits on a hillside overlooking the championship eighteen-hole Inverness Golf Course and the mountains to the west. The structure's gray and green exterior merges with both natural and built surroundings while marking its significance.

In plan, the design is an X anchored by a central, three-story, diamond-shaped atrium. To take complete advantage of the panoramic views, balconies positioned above the two wings face the mountains.

Trees were landscaped into the wedge-shaped exterior spaces created by the intersection of the wings. Multiplied and enhanced by reflections in the glass exterior walls, the trees create a visual forest.

This scheme was the first in the Rocky Mountain region to use a four-sided, structural silicone glazing system and among the first in the world to combine this technique with insulating vision glass. A structural silicone sealant was butt-jointed to each edge of the glass panels, eliminating visible exterior mullions and producing an uninterrupted surface of glass. This slick-tech exterior skin is constructed of alternating silver-reflective spandral glass panels and green insulated vision glass, creating a visual datum for each floor.

The building's parti also provides a creative context in which to present art. (An artist joined the design team.) The atrium, located in the building's center, is a separate space entirely enclosed by clear glass panels. This landscaped, skylit space functions as the building's main entrance and houses elevators as well as a series of cross-bridges that connect the four wings. Sculptures by artist Karl Rosenberg unify the entrance, lobby, and atrium. On each level, the elevator lobbies are flanked by additional skylit areas specifically designed for additional works of art.

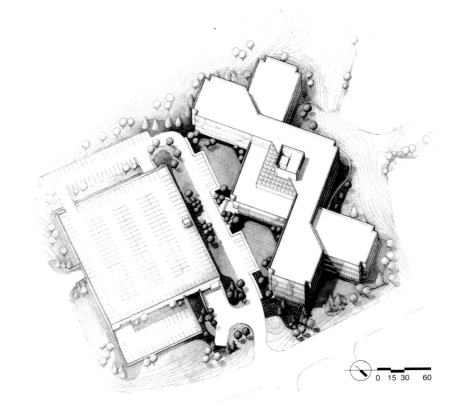

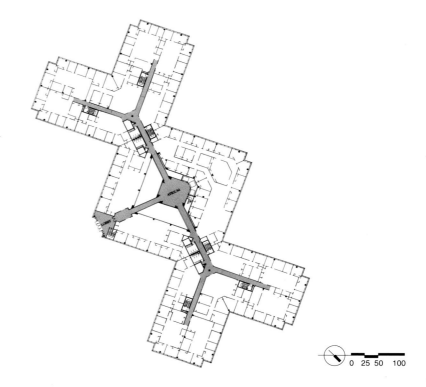

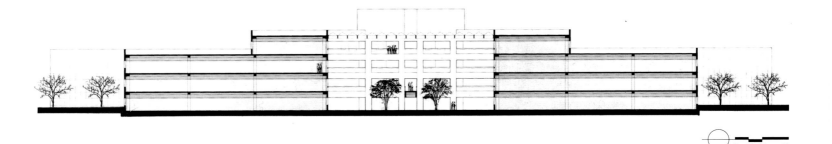

Milestone Square Master Plan

Englewood, Colorado

The Milestone Square master plan, a forty-eight-acre, seven-million-square-foot, mixed-use project, provides for the phased development of the site over a ten- to twenty-year period. Two clusters of four buildings are linked by a pedestrian spine that will house retail shopping, a fast-food court, restaurants, and adjacent parking facilities.

The form, height, and shape of the towers make a unique architectural statement, reducing the visual weight of the buildings while providing a dynamic appearance. The beveled corners and indented points that break up the mass of each tower create an illusion of four smaller, clustered ones.

Four structures are now complete: Milestone Tower, Terrace Tower II, and two detached parking structures.

The anchor of the master plan is the Milestone Tower. Originally designed to serve as the headquarters of Milestone Petroleum, this 240,000-square-foot, twelve-story Indiana limestone building is articulated as four terraced modules, each with chamfered corners and midpoint facade indentions that create the appearance of a double octagon. The cool, polished look of light grey granite walls and paving and a reflective stainless steel ceiling on the entry's interior are highlighted by an octagonal staircase and railing that lead down to a retail concourse one floor below. Atop the westernmost segment of the building, a landscaped restaurant terrace overlooks the panorama of downtown Denver and the mountains.

In this project, the firm explored current building technology, developing a post-tensioned limestone spandrel beam that carries the facade glazing. This was the first structural project in the world to use this technique.

The second phase of the project, Terrace Tower II, is identical to the first.

As a totality (plan, elevations, landscaping, and exterior materials), the Milestone Square complex will become a focus for the sprawling Denver Technological Center, which has no center.

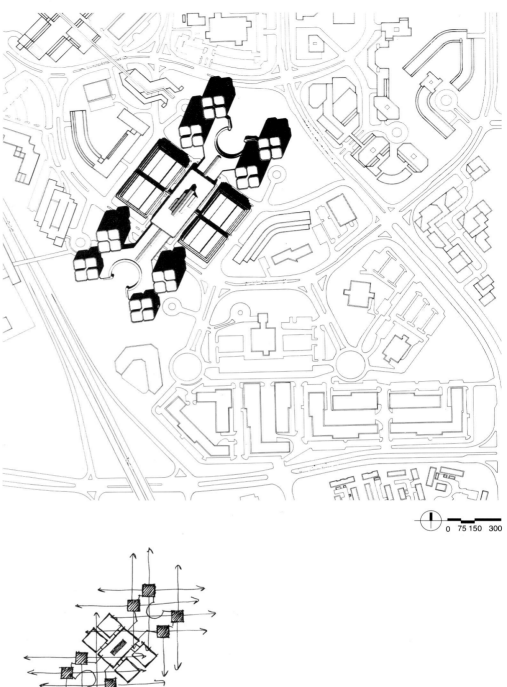

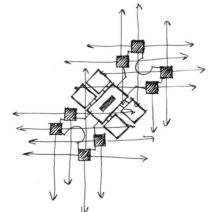

Kittredge Building

Denver, Colorado

Curtis Worth Fentress set the tenor of the preservation projects that the firm has executed to an extremely high standard. Each given structure had not only to be salvageable but to exhibit historical value as a design monument of its era. Such was the case with the firm's premier preservation project, the Kittredge Building.

Built in 1881 for Charles Marble Kittredge by architect A. Morris Stuckert, the Kittredge Building was Denver's first skyscraper. The Texas pink granite and rhyolite stone exterior, black with soot, had been remodeled in the 1950s, and much of its original detailing had been obscured or stripped. Thus, a first priority was to return the exterior to its original appearance. Cleaning and restoration revealed the richness of the original stone as well as the fine detailing unique to buildings of its time. Awnings were added once again to shade the ground floor windows.

The interior rehabilitation began with the lobby, which is now visible through a glass entrance set back from the original stone entry. The barrel-vaulted ceiling, which reinforced the shape of this original entry, was reconstructed and visually extended by a mirror placed over the elevators. In the new catalogue of luminaires for the lobby are a unique brass chandelier and cove lights concealed in a wood cornice that crowns the walls. Covering the lobby walls from floor to ceiling are quarter-sawn oak panels and fluted columns specially designed to recall the building's original wood detailing, which had been removed. The new flame-cut, pink granite paving matches the exterior stone.

The retail areas added in the 1950s were removed and the spaces redesigned into two restaurants: Goldie's (a New York delicatessen) and Marlowe's. Both serve theater patrons of the refurbished Paramount Theater, which occupies the other third of the building at street level.

All six floors of office space were completely reconstructed, adding contemporary HVAC, life-safety, and security systems without destroying the intricate visual aesthetic of the historic structure.

Each element of the preservation program ensures that the Kittredge Building remains as important a monument of design and technical advancement in the present as it was in the past.

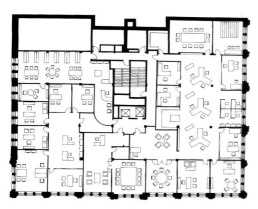

SECOND FLOOR PLAN

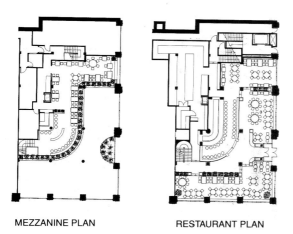

MEZZANINE PLAN   RESTAURANT PLAN

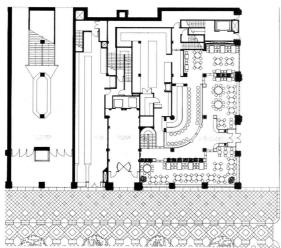

SIXTEENTH STREET PLAN   0 10 20 40

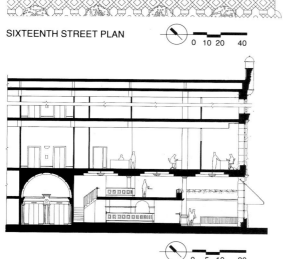

0 5 10 20

Museum of Western Art/
The Navarre

Denver, Colorado

This building's multifaceted and often crimson past first intrigued the designers. It coexisted with its neighbors, the Brown Palace Hotel and Trinity Methodist Church; while serving as a brothel the building had been linked by an underground tunnel to the hotel. This presented the firm with the additional conundrum of which layers to "strip off" to reveal the birth-skin of this nineteenth-century treasure. First constructed in 1880 as the Brinker Collegiate Institute, the Navarre changed hands many times. It was the Richelieu Hotel and later Peanuts Hucko's casino and bordello until the city outlawed gambling and prostitution in 1904. Eventually the structure was renamed after Henry of Navarre, a sixteenth-century French king, and gutted to be converted into office space and a restaurant. Purchased in 1983 by William Foxley with the intent of converting it into a private museum for his collection of western art, the structure, restored to its pristine and stately best, is listed on the National Register of Historic Places.

The completed museum, as designed by Fentress Bradburn in association with John Prosser, subtly accents Foxley's diverse collection of more than 125 paintings and sculptures.

The requirements of a contemporary museum housed within a landmark building led the architects to divide the Navarre vertically into two distinct sections, separated by a glass-enclosed stairway beneath the cupola and an adjacent elevator located within the building's core. The front lounge retains its historic character with finishes and period furniture selected to enhance its fin de siècle Victorian style, while the rear space was modified as the museum. The revised interior circulation plan permits a continuing procession of visitors to pass vertically through the stair core without constriction.

The new first floor gallery features a vaulted ceiling that, with its added height and indirect, diffused cove lighting, frames a zone for the exhibition of sculpture. Throughout the entire newly reorganized space, natural light has been reduced by erecting a secondary barrier several feet from the window wall. Low-wattage track lighting, which emits the least amount of harmful ultraviolet rays, is used as an alternative. In addition, special gallery lights are integrated into the articulated ceiling visually to enhance the building's original structural system.

Even in this preservation project, the firm deliberately addressed the philosophical issue of humanism by creating specific zones for contemplation and reflection to reduce the often confrontational nature of art and patron and to ease the fatigue of traversing multiple floors.

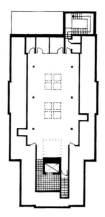

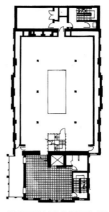

SECOND FLOOR PLAN

FOURTH FLOOR PLAN

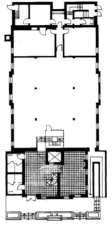

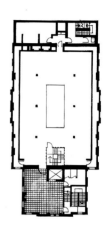

GROUND FLOOR PLAN

THIRD FLOOR PLAN

0 10 20 40

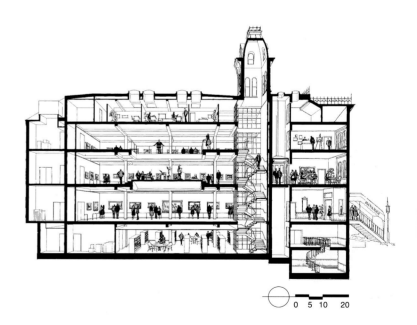

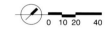

0 5 10 20

50

Odd Fellows Hall

Denver, Colorado

As an increasing number of structures of historical significance were razed in Denver's downtown urban corridor to make way for parking lots, Fentress Bradburn was applauded by the National Park Service for its preservation and restoration of the Odd Fellows Hall. Standing proudly and overlooking what has now become the all too familiar, gaped-toothed grin of the modern American metropolis, this diminutive building pleads its case for the continuity of good architecture and sound planning past and present.

Designed in 1889 by Emmet Anthony for the Odd Fellows Lodge, this meeting hall was centrally located in the downtown Denver business district. The original interior contained shops, a restaurant, offices, and a two-story meeting hall.

Although the exterior was deemed historically significant, and thus worth saving, the street facade was in an extremely battered condition. It was clear that this face would require a thorough restoration, but the architects wanted a complementary reinterpretation of the street-level facade to replace inappropriate storefronts that had been added over time.

The deteriorated interior was completely renovated for offices, retail shops, and restaurants. As the interior spaces were revised for better efficiency, a mezzanine and upper stories were added, as was a striking, curved glass-block elevator enclosure within a new, skylit atrium, and a basement-level interior courtyard restaurant, which opens upward through the atrium. The original interior featured coffered ceilings, mosaic tile flooring, bronze and marble finishes, and cherry millwork. The redesigned interior contains stylistically consistent and mimetic detailing.

The new retail shops and businesses located on the ground floor and the offices on the levels above recreate the elegant, nineteenth-century atmosphere of the original structure.

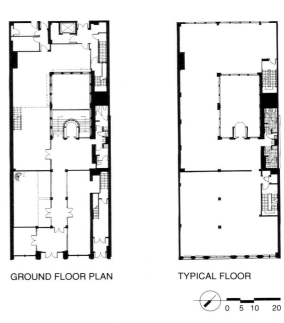

GROUND FLOOR PLAN   TYPICAL FLOOR

0 5 10 20

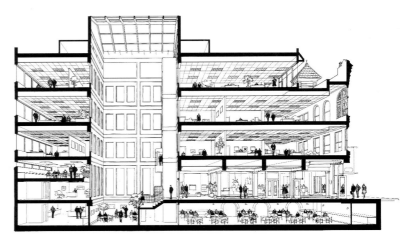

1999 Broadway

Denver, Colorado, 1985

The juxtaposition of sanctuary and skyscraper signifies the peaceful coexistence of two buildings whose historic symbiosis adds to the complexity of twentieth-century modernity. The green reflective glass and articulated limestone spandrels and columns accent the historic church while asserting the tower's corporate presence; together they symbolize the compressed rhythm of Denver's downtown cityscape.

Partially resting on fifty-foot columns, the tower interfaces with the church via a tall, stepped arcade that allows the church to remain physically independent and visually open. The resulting space offers complete circulation around both church and tower and creates two landscaped plazas for rest or contemplation.

Facing the house of worship, the house of commerce presents a concave wall that cradles the sanctuary and frames a view of the Rocky Mountains. On its opposite face, the tower's sharp corner cuts into the fabric of the city's central business district and presents a strong, contemporary corporate image.

Limestone was selected for the detailing because of its aesthetic qualities, long-term consistency of color, and durability. In addition, the stone echoes the church's brick and stone detailing.

This project is Fentress Bradburn's second application of a new technique for post-tensioned natural limestone beams.

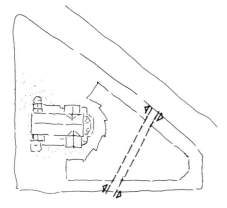

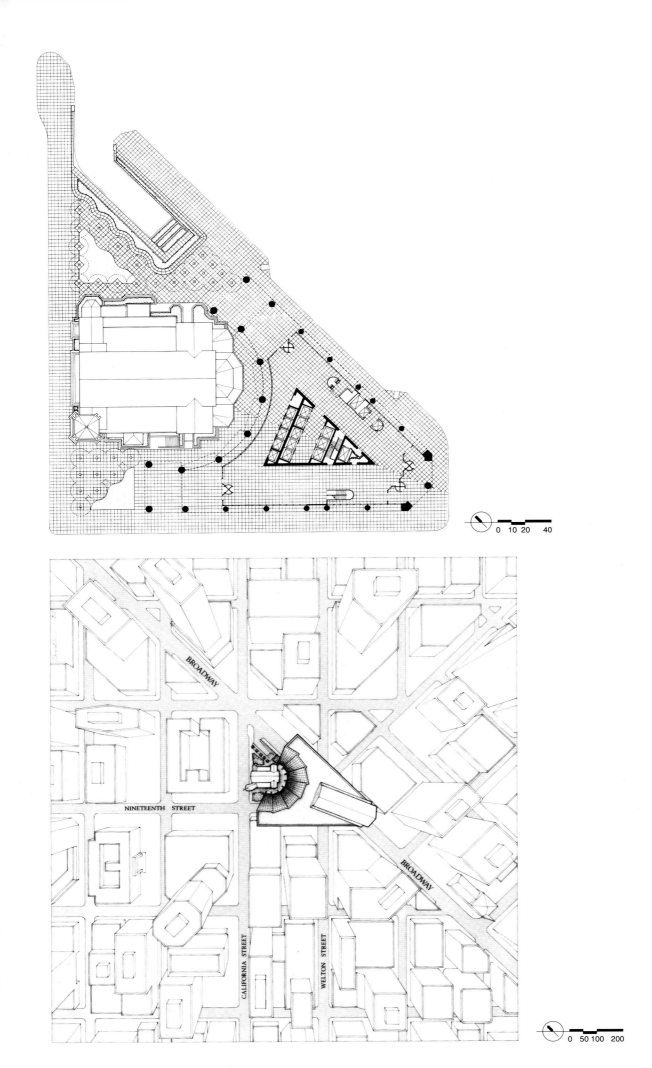

Holy Ghost Roman Catholic Church

Denver, Colorado

Since American urbanism began to concern itself with the preservation and gentrification of desired architectural forms, America past and contemporary have been juxtaposed in curious irony. Urban reuse and renewal often spare churches, synagogues, and cathedrals from demolition more than other pieces of the American mosaic. For example, the historic relevance of Holy Ghost Church was reconfirmed by the decision to retain its sense of place as an active parish within the context of an evolving site.

The decision to become involved in the inevitable changes that 1999 Broadway would bring to the site afforded the church an opportunity to continue its ministry while consciously sharing in its new environment.

Not only did the church directly influence the design of its surrounding built form; the church's aesthetic and functional qualities underwent an introspective design review process as well. This process involved elements seen and unseen. A fire-safety system, new wiring, a new heating system, and a below-grade addition contribute to the hidden value of the church as a temporal construct while securing its metaphysical purpose.

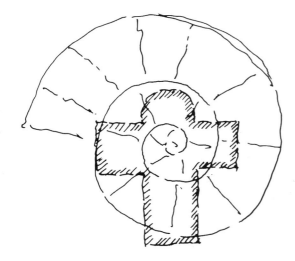

United Bank Tower

Tucson, Arizona

In the 1980s, politicians unconsciously promoted architecture that idealized American corporate life as they consciously sought to rejuvenate urban areas once fiscally abandoned. The American mecca of corporate architecture, New York City, had become quite crowded indeed, and the shifts in architectural culture from remove and rebuild to preserve and restore slowed the growth of Manhattan's island-bound skyline. The static result became an accepted collective iconography, a visual database desired by other American cities — particularly those in the Southwest. These structures, by embodying design ideas that assisted in making an American urban-economic core work, became an extended resource for corporate city planning in the 1980s.

Participating in this paradigm shift, United Bank Tower in Tucson, Arizona, embodies the new criteria of the village aping the metropolis. Part one of a two-part project, this twenty-three-story tower rises above the other structures composing Tucson's downtown. The project was deliberately designed to catalyze an extensive redevelopment plan for Tucson's central business district. This ideal was then coupled with other, more tangible interests paramount to redefining the economic center.

Bordering the downtown district is the architecture of a different America. Both stylized and legitimate veins of Spanish mission architecture fueled this project's skin and overall aura. To create a more human scale, the block itself was bisected with a walkway allowing for more interesting figure-field relationships, instead of the inappropriate and purely pragmatic solution of covering the whole site with building.

The tower's interior functions permit a hierarchy of business to occur on a regular basis. Neo-Renaissance space planning subtly integrates piano-nobile and street-level functions while the stories above accommodate business operations.

The decorative scheme, full of contrast and vibrancy, takes its inspiration from the region's earthy landscape, incorporating the blues of the night sky and the oranges of the desert sunset. The pink and red desert earth finds reflection in the polished granite of the banking hall and lobby.

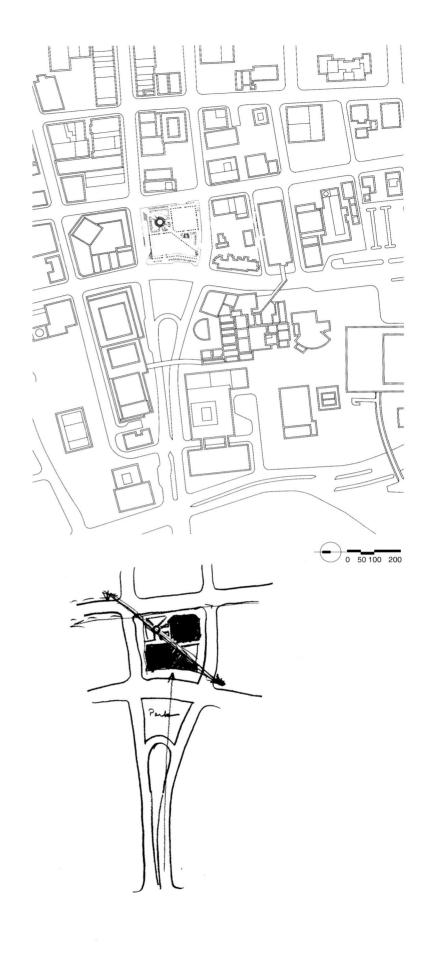

0 50 100 200

The facade of a building is often more important than its plan. Architecture is not only about signs and sign systems, but facades immediately orient the user. The building may remain an object, but facade readability triggers understanding of what lies within. The facade of the Idaho Power Company subtly reveals a comforting and symmetrical enclosure.

This nine-story building, the initial phase of a master plan for the Idaho Power Company corporate headquarters, exploits a stylistic collision of mid-modernism and a Corbusian classicism as a means of orientation. Not unlike the facade of a Gothic cathedral, where the entrance is articulated by the relationships of surrounding forms, proportional fenestration and a *brise-soleil* here frame the main entry. Reiteration of the classical mode of arranging the office tower like a column, from base to shaft to capital, further enhances the overall composition.

Thus, structure and skin act respectively as object and subject in relation to a first-phase requirement: the headquarters building will inform the subsequent developments by providing an integral node on which to grow.

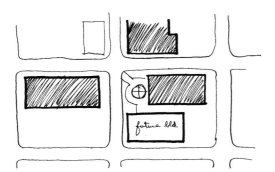

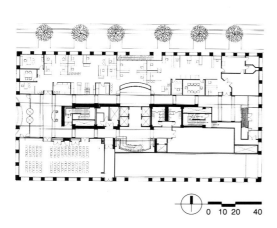

Denver Permit Center

Denver, Colorado

Denver, Colorado, much like other urban American experiments, has weathered the paradigm shifts of architecture, design, and civic identity. Its public architecture, like that of the American political structure in general, is predominately neoclassical in origin. Seen by many as both historicist and revivalist, this stylistic approach is distinctive in a rich and peculiar way but has left few postmodern monuments.

One such postmodern gesture is the renovation and transformation of an outmoded, relatively nondescript university law library from the earlier modern era into a government data processing center. The interior of the new Denver Permit Center was redesigned as an elegant frame for the occupant, with the installation of a four-story atrium as the central gathering and orientation node. The exterior skin was reworked to reflect the American neoclassicism of Denver's civic center while emphasizing the bold curves of the adjacent modernist Denver Art Museum.

The building's orientation was reconfigured to create a clearer understanding of its parti and to introduce a human scale lacking in the grandiose neoclassicism of its civic companions. Thus one corner of the structure is emphatically delineated by a portico/rotunda. More than a superficial gesture, this corner/facade acts as an architectural narthex, a point of collision between city and structure. Housed within this space is a metaphorical sculpture, allowed simultaneously by the popularized discourse of Jacque Derrida and Denver's one-percent-for-art program. The carefully staged relationship between sculpture and architecture marks the rise of postmodernism and deconstruction.

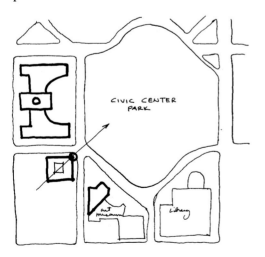

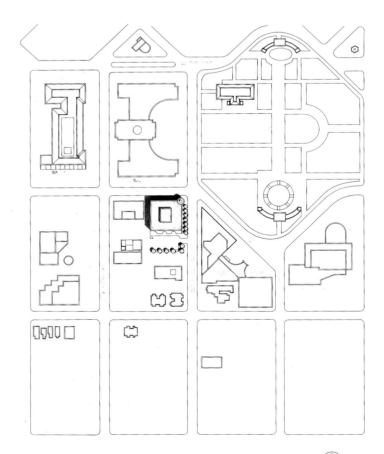

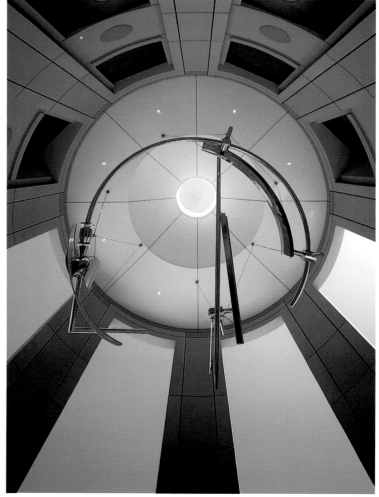

Jefferson County Government Center
Master Plan
Golden, Colorado

The popularized discourse of complexity and contradiction in architectural theory and practice might have seemed plausible were it not for the voids in the discussion that demand unique attention. By accepting American strip culture as a two-dimensional system of signs and symbols, with the automobile as the dominant threshold and humankind as a mere consumer, many American cities developed the condition labeled "sprawl": an urban evolution correctly identified as mechanized, nonorganic viral clustering. Approaching the uninhabitable, sprawl has fractured cities by eroding urban centers and disbursing the fragments to multiple locales. Such was the case with Jefferson County, Colorado.

Perched on the edge of the Denver metropolis, and reacting to its influence, Jefferson County had evolved no center. Its innards had been scattered randomly over a wide and demographically diverse geography. Here, as in other American cities, more intimate pockets of development and redevelopment essentially had reacted to the dominant cult of the automobile.

Motivated by a philosophical shift in urban planning ideals in the late 1970s, planners gradually engaged the automobile, and its overshadowing of most principal aspects of American culture, in tangible experiments in controlled breakdown theory and a phenomenon called flexible accumulation. Malls, civic complexes, and edge cities became design excursions for architects and planners alike, who concerned themselves with developing an extra-human utopia. However, given the extra-human factor in the very human desire for utopia, architects and planners invented subtle ways to deemphasize the more frenzied qualities of the machine culture. Thus, the Jefferson County Government Center is master planned to function as an architectural filtering system by combining design principles responsive to the gathering and distribution of culture and the administration of local government.

In this instance, architecture and landscape are considered together. Open space was recognized as an existing proto-form in need of articulation. To keep pace with the complexities of civic functions and the rapid rate of growth and economic exchange in Jefferson County, the design solution addresses the compilation of new facilities for human resources, public parks, and regulatory processing, made manifest by layering discourse, need, and spatial experience.

These concerns are realized in a grand yet intimate scale. The Human Services Building and the Courts and Administration Building are aesthetically enticing as they dismiss the notion that civic architecture must overwhelm. Design concepts geared toward human beings facilitate such a shift.

Spaces in the Human Services Building house counseling and other services while allowing enough openness to encourage those in need to participate more readily. Instead of unfriendly barriers, carefully placed glass partitions achieve a more gentle separation. Fenestration also plays a key role by affording most rooms views, unlike many civic buildings that reflect older social values by secreting such activities.

The circulation halls in the Courts and Administration Building evoke the pomp and circumstance associated with such procedures. However, alcoves rhythmically placed on the interior side of the halls provide relief from the public way for brief moments of privacy.

Glimpses and vistas through carefully placed trees and orientation at the point of destination recall early American picturesque efforts such as the winding approach road at Washington's Mount Vernon.

The Jefferson County complex's harmonious and refined coloration relies on hues and variations found in the surrounding front-range landscape. Wheat-colored brick matches the clay in the foothill hogbacks, and the bands of deep maroon granite were inspired by the surrounding soil and indigenous sandstone.

Thus, this new complex reestablishes the symbolic importance of a county seat while creating a geographic center that generates an increased sense of community.

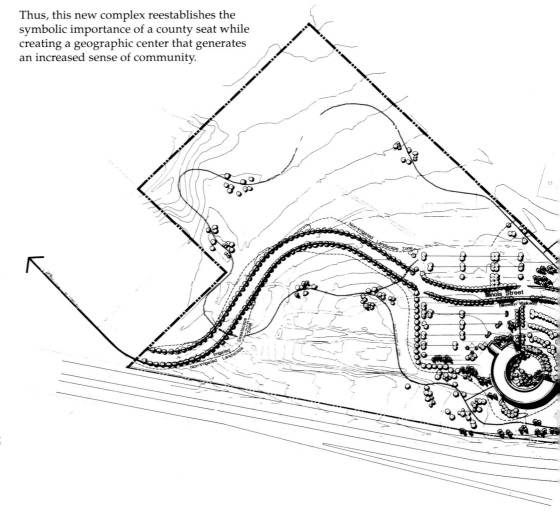

outdoor
theater
site

future bbb site

open space

open space

Highway 470

Wier Street

Irrigation Streetscape

Parkway Trail

County Parkway

W. 10th Avenue Realignment

Broad Parkway

Irrigation Streetscape

Secondary Trail

0 75 150 300

Human Services Building

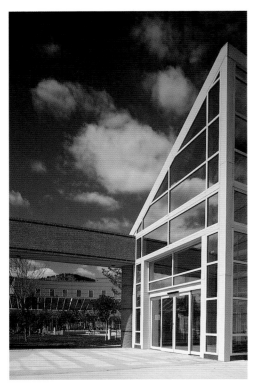

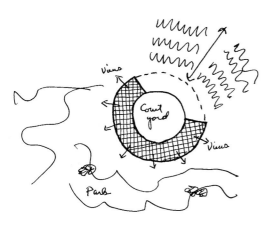

Courts and Administration Building

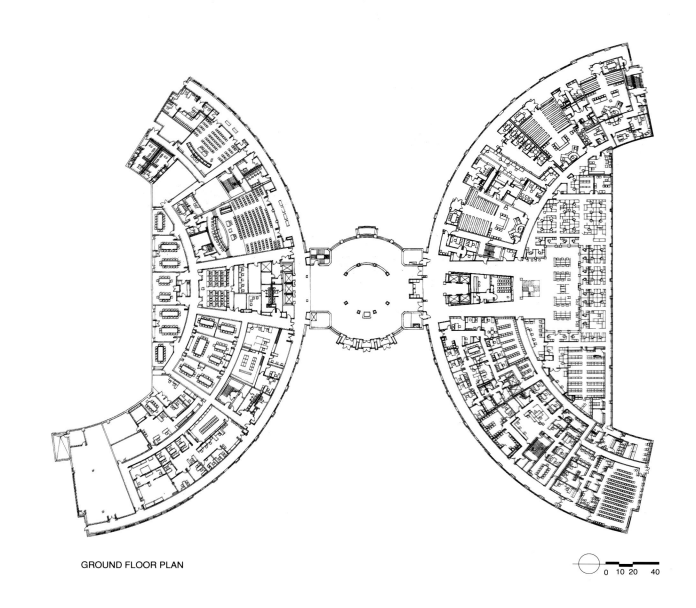

GROUND FLOOR PLAN

0 10 20 40

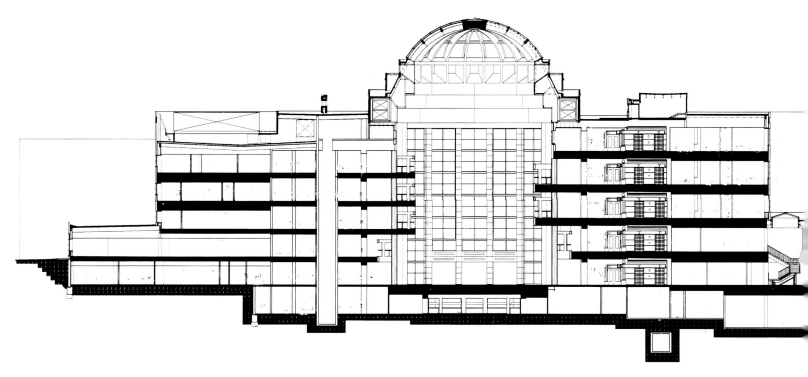

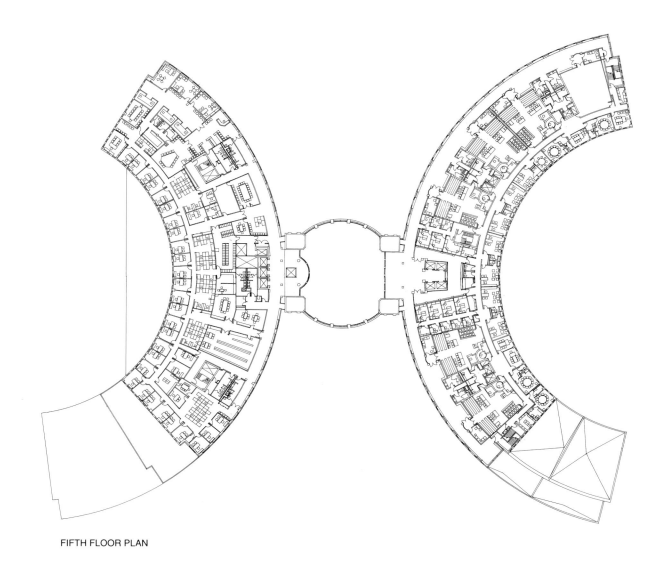

FIFTH FLOOR PLAN

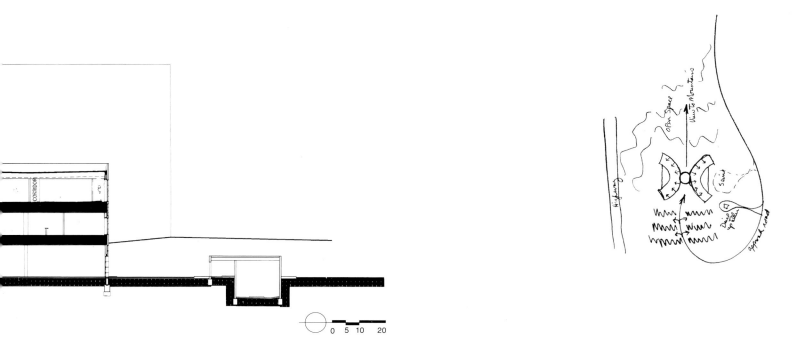

0 5 10 20

Colorado Convention Center

Denver, Colorado

Postmodern building occasionally reflects the processes that bring it about. Conceptually, postmodern imagery results when formerly normative architectural ideas are manipulated, reversed, or inverted to reflect the modernist dictum "less is more."

At the Colorado Convention Center this ideal was carried through multiple design phases in spite of pressure from governmental entities. Thus, the architects were afforded frequent opportunities to design afresh as the public committee's architectural ideals changed rapidly. However, primary architectural and structural motifs remained undisturbed, carrying the essence and meaning of the building.

Thresholds here are strong, distinguished from the rest of the form through curved, exploding structural *arrivés* that serve as cultural gateways between the city proper and the peaked landscape to the west, gesturally displaying the unique pioneering spirit of the American mercantile.

The interior contains the grand spaces that accommodate the needs of the new American business pastime, the convention, which essentially synthesizes elements from the earlier world expositions.

Here is the first American convention center in which synthesis of interior and exterior space is treated as a commodity: the interior contains massive halls with grand and convenient circulation patterns while exterior greenspace can accommodate overflow as an outdoor hall.

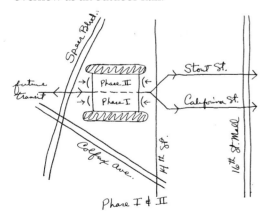

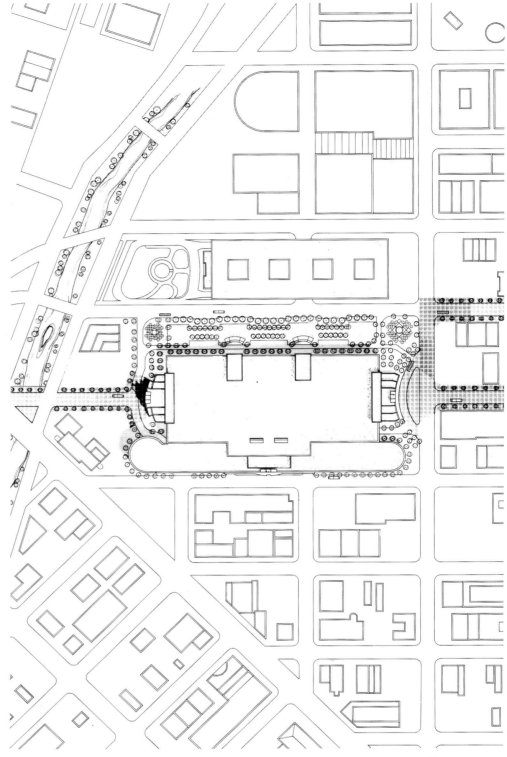

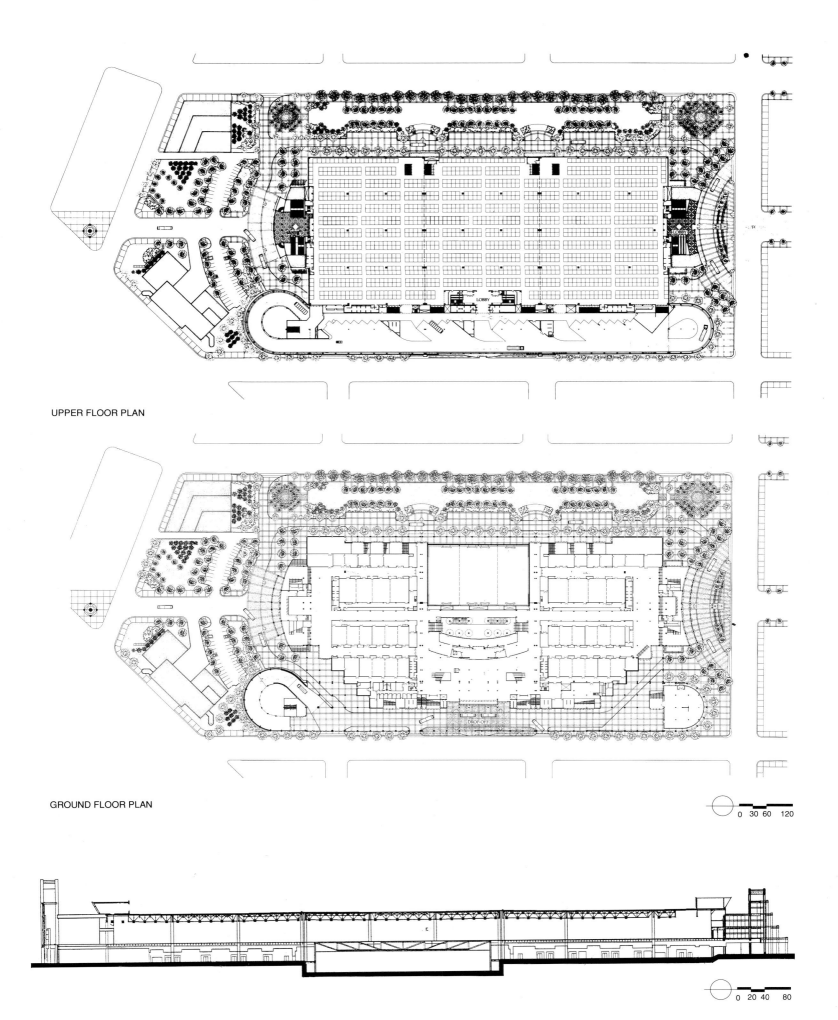

UPPER FLOOR PLAN

GROUND FLOOR PLAN

0 30 60   120

0 20 40   80

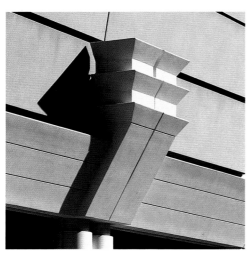

Ronstadt Transit Center

Tucson, Arizona

The universality of travel in late modern American culture often lends itself to forms that constitute functionally engineered non-architecture. When functionality is understood as more than banal, however, the idea of marking activity revitalizes architecture. The Ronstadt Transit Center in Tucson, Arizona, exhibits such functional, provisional architecture, human in scale and sensation. Acting as a standard hub for the city, the center permits transitional, alternative, and continuing modes of transportation. The center accommodates travelers while dispelling contemporary urban stereotypes about the bus terminal.

Travel destinations were marked repeatedly in Western societies of the late nineteenth to early twentieth centuries by grand Beaux-Arts complexes. These complex forms occasionally derived from Roman bathhouses, which were primarily chosen for their ability to accommodate the masses. The bathhouse type also conveyed a grandiose sense of permanence while allowing the beneficial elements of light and air to intermingle with the occupants. Similar considerations motivated the design of the Ronstadt Transit Center. Light and air participate as a functional part of the design. Plantings and simplified shelter forms provide protection from the sun while two cooling towers, based on centuries-old wind towers in the Middle East, employ technology developed at the University of Arizona Environmental Research Laboratory to water-cool hot, dry air and make it available to those occupying the space below. A typical Tucson summer temperature can rise to 114 degrees Fahrenheit; these evaporative cooling towers lower the temperature ten to fifteen degrees within a twenty-foot radius.

A sense of place is achieved through the integration of local recycled brick and tiles created by a local artist. These play familiar revivalist-decorative roles, as such elements often did in the more expansive transportation halls of yesteryear.

Here also the deliberate application of scientific color theory invokes a sense of safety and harmony and in turn discourages the crime often associated with urban transportation centers.

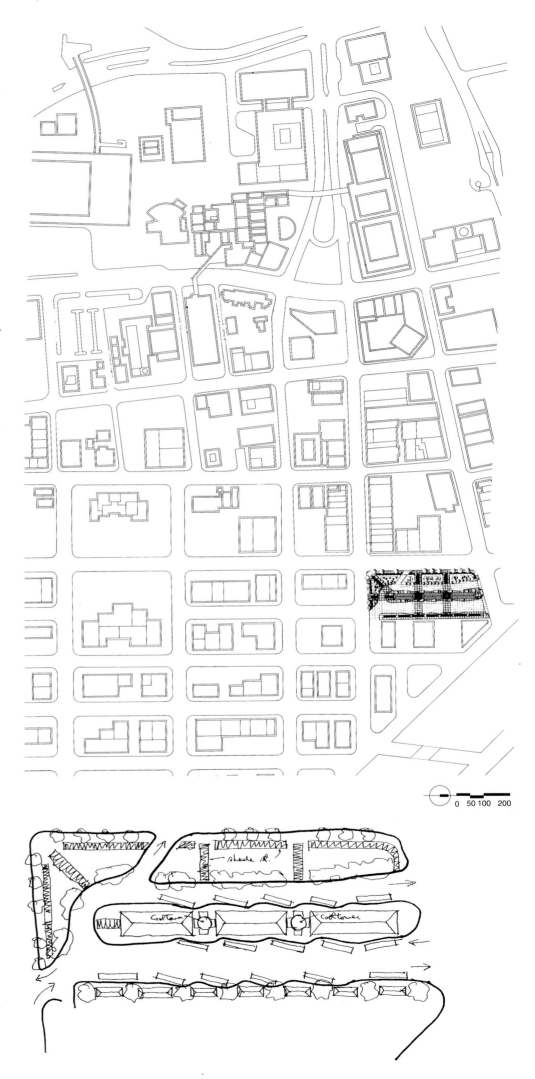

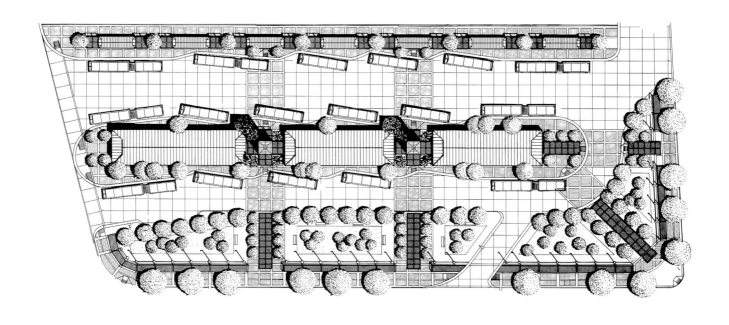

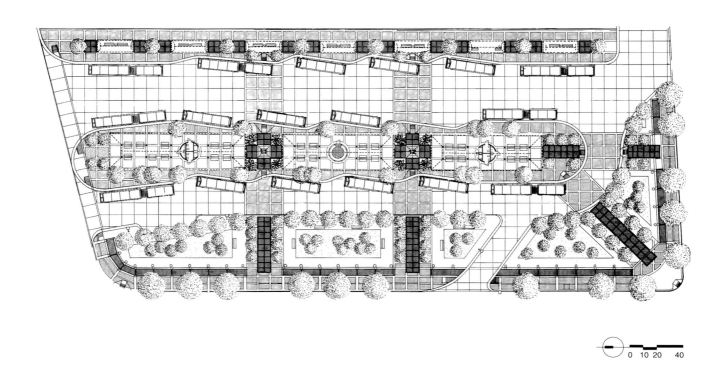

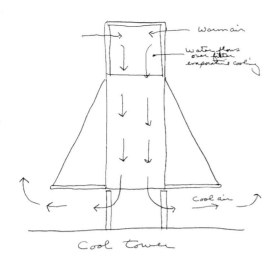

Warm air

Water flows
over filter
evaporative cooling

Cool air

Cool tower

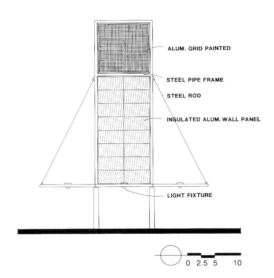

ALUM. GRID PAINTED

STEEL PIPE FRAME

STEEL ROD

INSULATED ALUM. WALL PANEL

LIGHT FIXTURE

0 2.5 5   10

Gemmill Mathematics Library
and Engineering Sciences Building

Boulder, Colorado

Keeping within the bounds of Charles Klauder's and Hideo Sasaki's master plans for the University of Colorado at Boulder (dating from 1917 and 1960, respectively), the Gemmill Mathematics Library and Engineering Sciences Building subtly accommodates the urban visual tension created by our not so distant modern past.

Valued functional architectural icons, such as the eighty-foot campanile and low-running loggias, are programmed to connect and direct a network of open greens, quadrangles, and strong axial pathways. The design composite is essentially comprised of figure-field relationships suitably stretched into four thin, distinct cloistered and open horizontal layers.

Programmatic elements have been neatly arranged to accommodate the needs of the complex. They include the Gemmill Mathematics Library located below grade and the new mathematics offices and facility commons room above grade. These components are abutted by a four-hundred-seat auditorium and the Excaliburlike presence of the four-story campanile.

Blending the modernist standard of the 1960s and early seventies with Klauder's revivalist, early twentieth-century rural Italian Tuscan style, the project envelops an architecturally trying proposition evidenced in both the varied forms and mixed materials. Native sandstone exteriors and clay tile roofs are used in conjunction with precast concrete to suggest a new postmodern ideal.

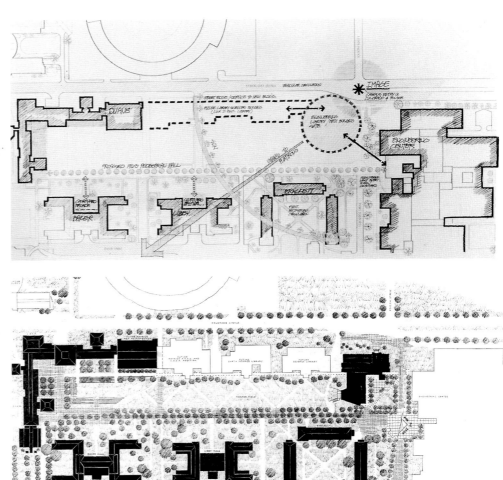

NORTH ELEVATION

SOUTH ELEVATION

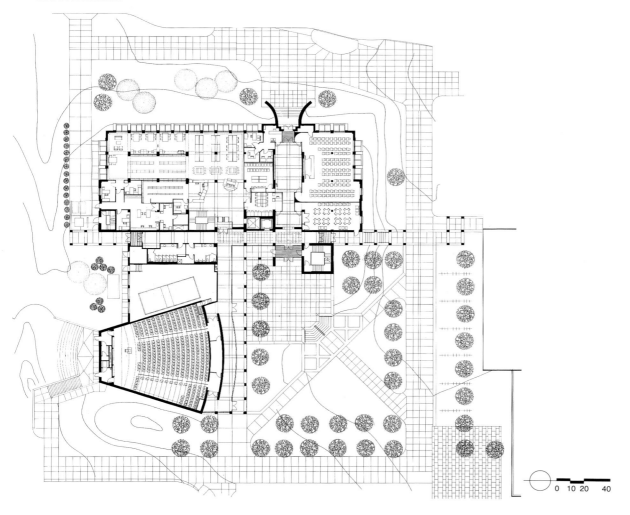

0 10 20 40

Natural Resources Building

Olympia, Washington

The Natural Resources Building is located on the east campus of the state capitol in Olympia, Washington. This departmental building houses the three state agencies of Natural Resources, Fisheries, and Agriculture. The complex is comprised of office and laboratory space and a 1,360-vehicle parking garage.

The dramatic curve of the facade is derived from the inscribed geometry of the central civic center campus emanating from the capitol building. The form acts as a terminus for the north side of the campus and anchors the east campus while recalling the rhythm and texture of the traditional structures of the west campus.

The landscaping recreates the richness of Washington's ecology, including its forest and wetlands, by depicting patterns of beach, cobbled shore, marsh, grassland, and forest fringe.

The focal point of the building is a rotunda offset from the main body of the building but centered on the campus grid. This towered atrium frames and terminates the east campus axis, directly referencing the capitol building as an axis pin. The building entry through the atrium presents visitors and employees alike with an internal point of orientation just as its external figural form offers focus and orientation within the campus.

The architectural detail of the rotunda, linked to the landscape vocabulary of Washington, graphically expresses the essence of the three agencies housed within.

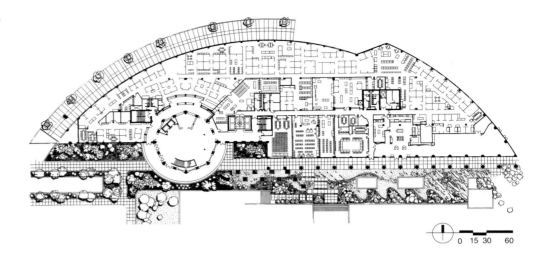

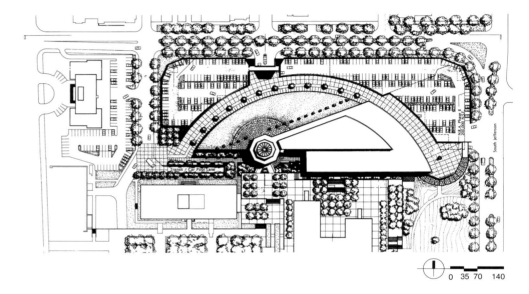

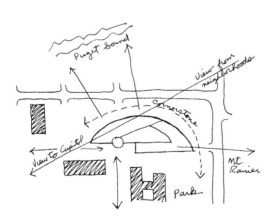

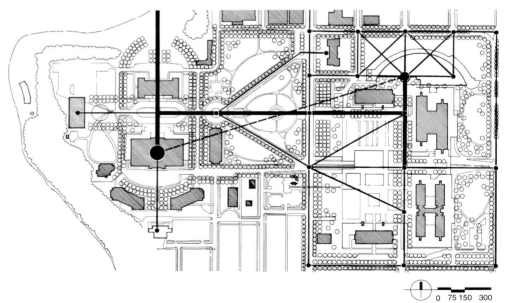

PREVAILING WINDS ARE USED TO
AID IN VENTILATION OF THE BUILDING

SEPARATE SWITCHING OF LAMPS ALLOWS
LUMINAIRES TO BE ADJUSTED TO PROVIDE
1/3, 2/3 OR FULL LIGHT LEVELS

PERIMETER LIGHT SYSTEMS SWITCHED
INDEPENDENTLY FROM INTERIOR SPACES

ENERGY EFFICIENT EIFS BUILDING SKIN
WITH R-VALUES RANGING FROM
A MINIMUM OF R-12 UP TO R-35

ANALOG LIGHT SENSORS IN THE SPACE
MONITOR LIGHT LEVELS, AND IN CONJUNCTION
WITH A CAMPUS WIDE MONITORING SYSTEM ALLOW
FOR OPTIMAL LIGHTING LEVELS
AND ENERGY EFFICIENCY

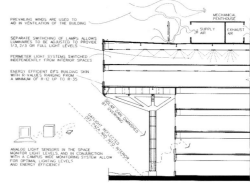

Denver International Airport
Passenger Terminal Complex

Denver, Colorado

Architects, designing toward the twenty-first century, have moved beyond the synoptic discourse of postmodernism and are now developing a transcendent, other than modern, other than postmodern synthesis of art and engineering. In the Denver International Airport this process is modified by the knowledge that for decades visionaries and futurists have seen the airport as a primary center, even a definer, of culture.

Removing responsibility for such architectural events from the hands of purely functionalist engineers has provoked architects and visionaries to revitalize interest in the terminal type. Not since Eero Saarinen have architects worked in this realm with such vigour, which demands definitive architectural skills at a high level of programmatic intensity. A new building type is being regenerated that defines itself as a bird's-eye portal, a gateway, and a threshold to be experienced as much from above as from on the ground. Denver International Airport accomplishes this post-postmodern synthesis.

Denver's mayor Federico Peña sought a design that would create an iconographic symbol of Denver much like that of the Opera House in Sydney, Australia. The relationship between the tensile-membrane structure and the activity of modern life within and around it illustrates the intertextual megapolis that airports become. The airport offers a refractive image of how the city of Denver, a complex cosmopolitan node, exists within its unique surroundings of two romanticized American landscapes (awe-inspiring mountains and vast, open prairies).

The tensile-membrane roof offers a figurative and literal focus. Even the way in which light is absorbed, emitted, and omitted metaphorically articulates its architectural function. The mammoth scale suggests an awakening giant, a memorable threshold.

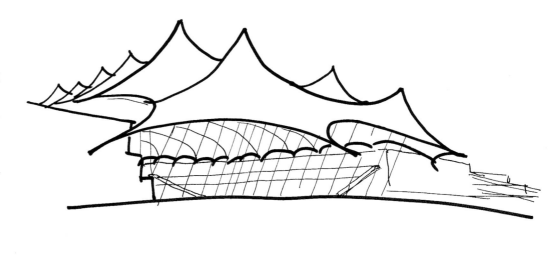

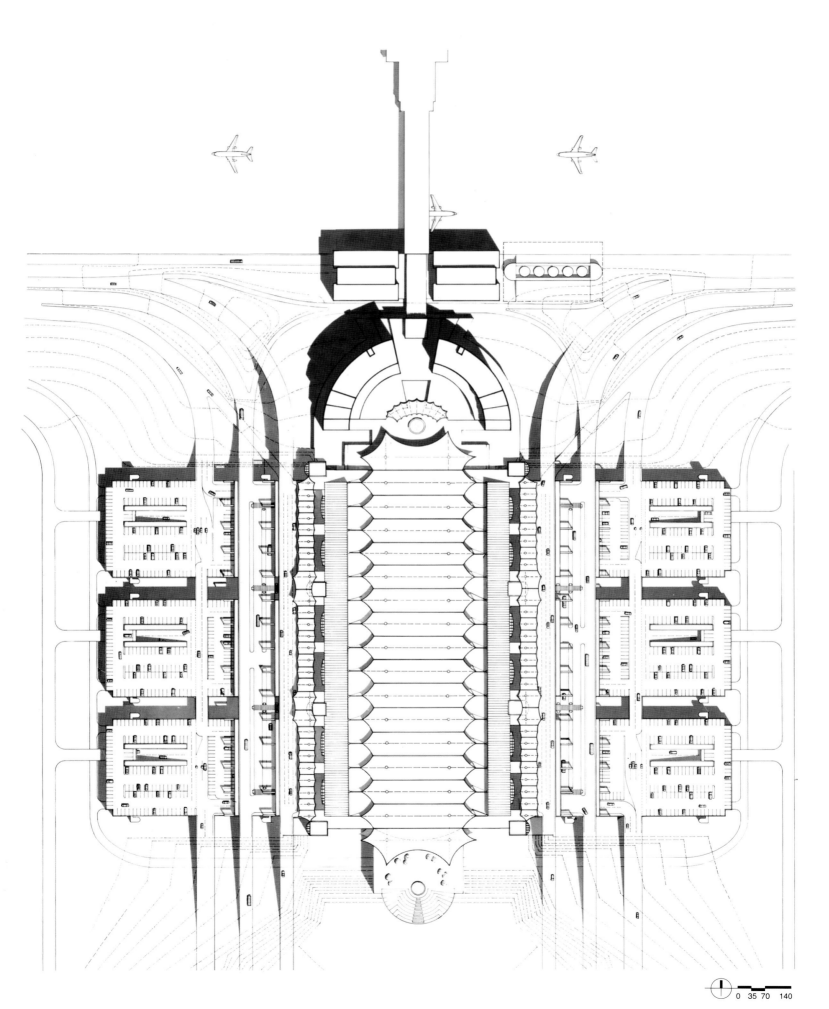

WEST ELEVATION

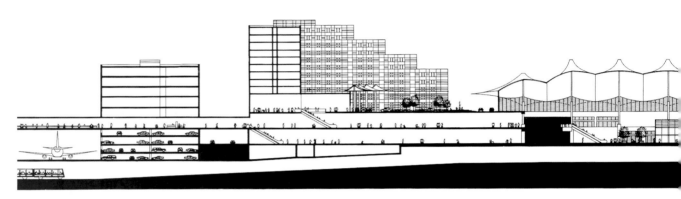

LONGITUDINAL SECTION

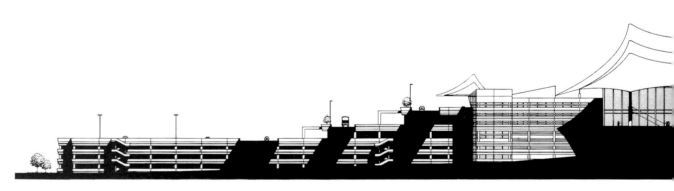

SOUTH ELEVATION

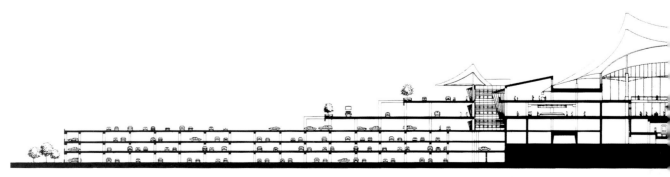

CROSS SECTION

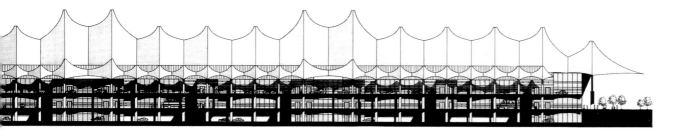

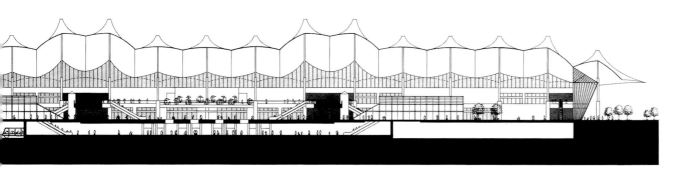

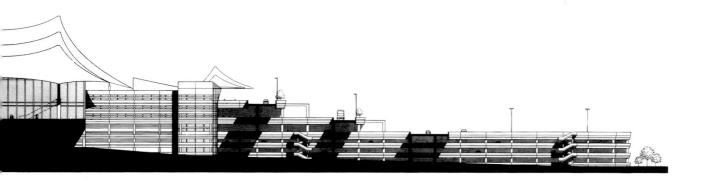

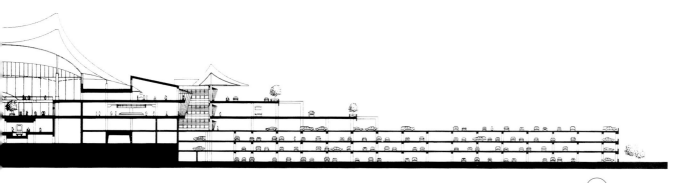

0 15 30   60

SELECTED WORKS

In Design

Ogden-Weber State University Conference and Performing Arts Complex

Ogden, Utah

Urban decay has become endemic to American culture. As the built environment ages, its elegance is consumed by neglect or indifference until portions either crumble or are removed, often leaving gaps in the fabric that was once the city. This phenomenon affects every American town down to the smallest rural villages. The effect in Ogden, Utah, however, is markedly different, and reworking this town fabric carried the potential to create interesting new forms.

By the time city planning became reality in the far Midwest, organizational civic ideals, ranging from the structured western grid to the absolutism of regulated style, had gained a significant foothold. Many of these townships are now being shaped by postmodern Violet-le-Ducs and their idealistic resurrection and resuscitation of older built forms, without consideration of the possibilities of creating something new and unique from the old fabric. Many different urban agglomerations are being reconstructed, and Fentress Bradburn believes that each requires unique treatment. Revitalizing Ogden's Egyptian revival-style theater, the former center for the performing arts, involved applying significant new layers to generate an architectural identity that is something quite more than its predecessor. What emerged is a multipurpose civic center. This new combination engages in design/nondesign synergy, where the acceptance of previously built elements directs the visual focus toward new elements that add to the quality of the whole. By engaging older forms with respect, new forms themselves gain respect. The sum is the new life.

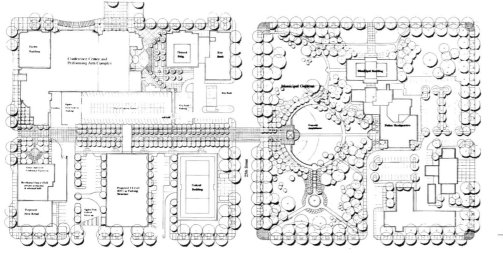

0 50 100 200

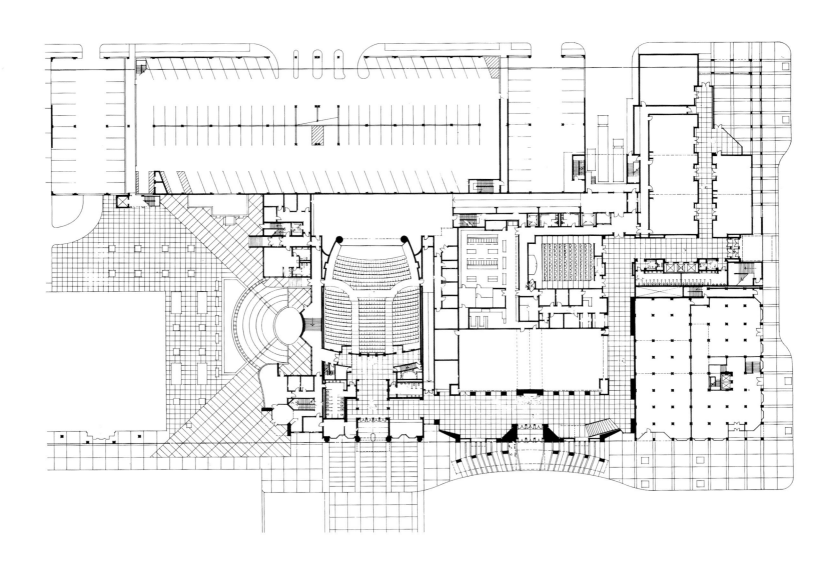

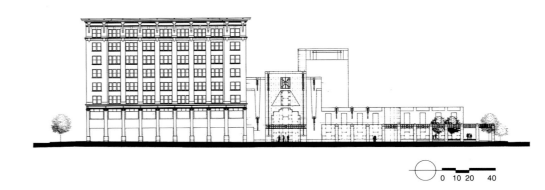

0 10 20   40

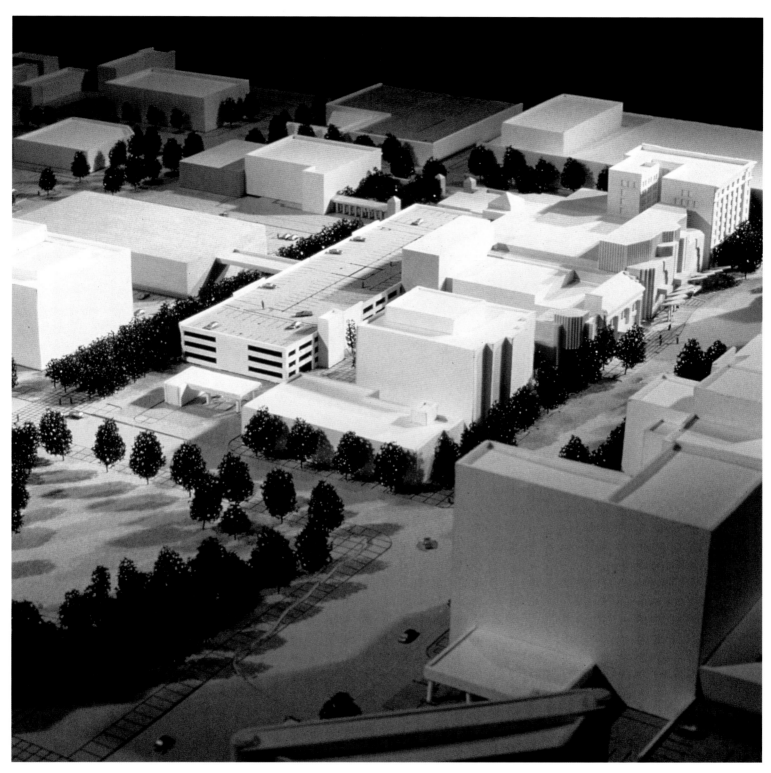

National Cowboy Hall of Fame

Oklahoma City, Oklahoma

Growth (and all of the pains that go along with it) is a celebrated event within most aspects of western culture. Subtle changes are often marked with architectural gestures that tie what was to the present and define what is to come. In this way, growth provides the opportunity to reaffirm place within schematic spaces.

Architectural growth is not without its pains. Often, the functions of a building outgrow its form. The National Cowboy Hall of Fame in Oklahoma City, Oklahoma, is one such example. This well-marked structure provided Fentress Bradburn the opportunity to test the tangential relationship of architectural theory to practice within the problematic context of growth.

Satisfying the need for more gallery and museum space, low-level building forms are tucked carefully behind existing structures. These additions provide clear circulation as well as a more suitable environment for display of the hall's collections.

The expansion/renovation program considers the transition of the visitor from the adjacent interstate highway, for example, which mandated a complete reconsideration of the natural environment as enclosure and the addition of dynamic built elements to enhance curiosity.

Much of the image for the National Cowboy Hall of Fame is defined by Leonard McMurray's *Buffalo Bill Memorial*. While strategically placed to take full advantage of its scale, the sculpture's present color and surrounding vegetation diminish the visual impact on visitors drawn from the highway. The sculpture's impact will be enhanced by a dramatic "floating" white backdrop that recalls the existing architecture and reinforces the new entry to the museum. This new entry is anchored by a sweeping curved canopy that gathers people in a welcoming gesture. The canopy reinforces a sense of entry lost in the original plan and aligns the visitor with one of the strengths of the existing complex, the reflecting pool and sculpture garden beyond.

This singular stroke of reinstating the *Buffalo Bill Memorial* as the dominant element in the landscape deifies the quintessential image of cowboy culture itself while redefining the importance of Oklahoma City as center of such historic culture.

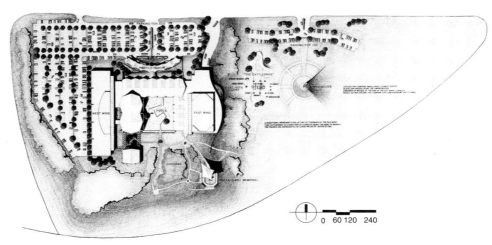

0   60 120   240

0 10 20   40

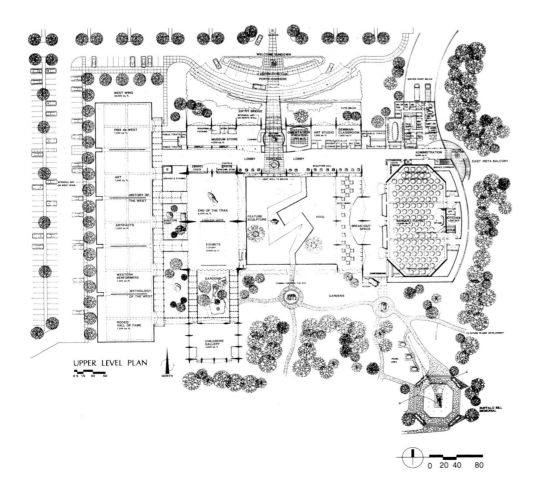

UPPER LEVEL PLAN

0 5 15   30   50

NORTH

0 20 40   80

National Oceanic and Atmospheric Administration Headquarters

Boulder, Colorado

The nature of university burroughs and the potential intermingling with newer economic forces in American culture has resulted in an adjunct urbanism known as the "research park," the information age's version of the modern industrial complex. Many of these parks encompass prior urban densities, absorbing, figuratively and literally, entities such as universities, high-tech companies, research centers, and smaller industrial parks. Within this new paradigm, some of the newest ideas in art, history, and criticism are knowingly and unknowingly communicated.

Broader urban formations (which transcend traditional ideas of the city) such as Boulder, Colorado, the site of this design, are intentionally, wonderfully complex and politically challenging resources. Here exists a library of ideas that challenges architects to embark on ventures that could redefine American culture.

The National Oceanic and Atmospheric Administration Headquarters responds to Boulder by revitalizing the advantages of centrality for closely related fields of research: aeronomy, climate monitoring, air resources, forecast systems, national severe storms tracking, space environment, national weather service wave propagation, national geophysical data, and mountain administration support, all in relation to its University of Colorado neighbor and predecessor, the National Center for Atmospheric Research. The facility is further integrated into its environment by interaction between the building's modulating lab-block forms, whose scale and beveling refer to the table mesa residential neighborhood and its geography. The complex also generates a series of frames that graciously pay tribute to Boulder's picturesque icon, the Flat Irons geological formation.

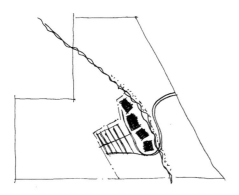

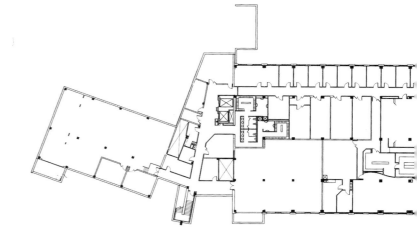

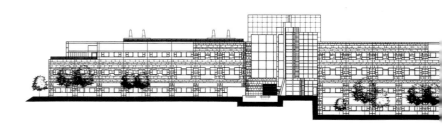

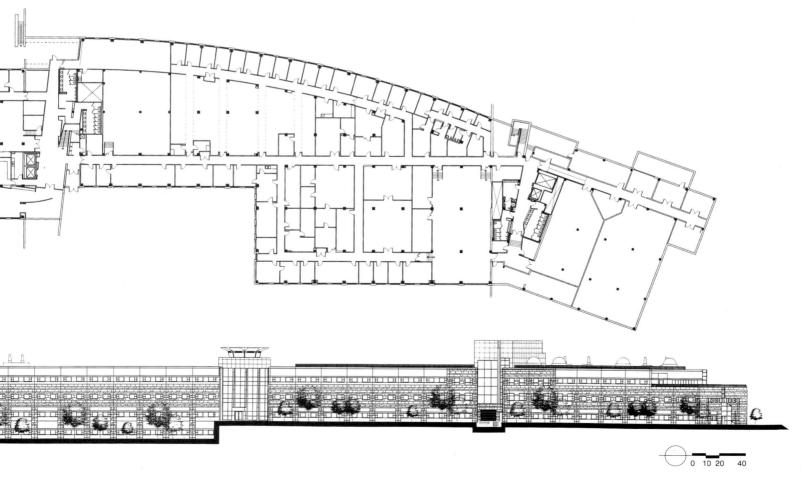

0 10 20   40

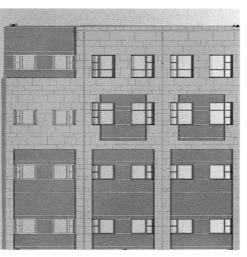

Clark County
Government Center

Las Vegas, Nevada

Inspired by the desert environment of Clark County, Nevada, the Clark County Government Center makes a distinctive architectural statement that responds to the natural and man-made, contemporary and historical ecology of the region.

As the canyon walls serve as a backdrop and form giver to the desert floor, the government center similarly delineates this civic place. Its amphitheater, ringed with a dense network of deciduous trees, offers areas of public shade and oasis planes of grass for contemplation; the cafeteria echoes the remains of geologically formed pyramids rising out of the desert floor. The commissioner's chamber auditorium incorporates an intricate network of skylights that recall the familiar prickly pear cactus. Resembling the strata along canyon walls, the amphitheater skin spirals upward and wraps the building's entry, framing the county room as the focal point of the composition. The entrance promenade provides a natural ceremonial passageway as sandstone remnants determine movement across the desert. The campus plan resembles an ancient wall carving, an image of Nevada's cultural heritage recorded in petroglyphs.

The arrangement of the complex offers a clear diagram, a series of places and events surrounding the exterior public space of the county courtyard. An *alleé* serving as a pedestrian spine establishes the boundary between the government complex and the desert while directing visitors to the courtyard. The organization of volumes within the primary building provides clarifying direction. For example, as citizens traverse the ground and second levels, the county courtyard is clearly visible outside, thus establishing orientation.

This complex embraces and welcomes the visitor with the outstretched arms of its inscribed structural form, providing the impression of an open and accessible government for the citizens it serves.

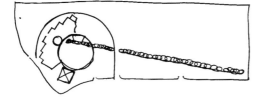

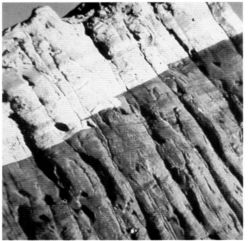

177

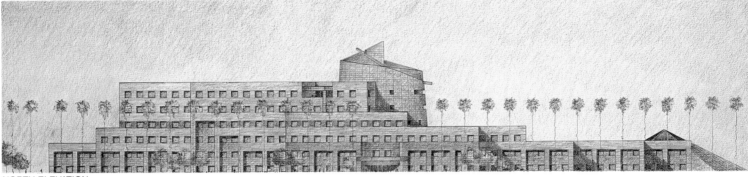

NORTH ELEVATION

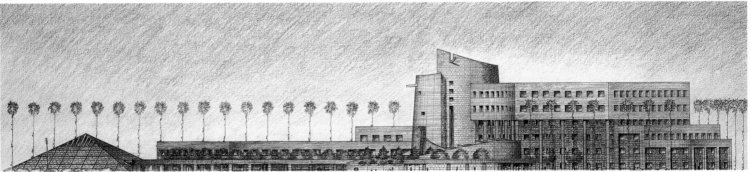

SOUTH ELEVATION

0 10 20   40

National Museum of Wildlife Art

Jackson Hole, Wyoming

Contemporary society's quest to integrate the artificial and the natural invites the architect to address this new type of political correctness. However, as the debate progresses, the appropriate sensitive interaction between natural and built appears less and less intangible, and its apparent irresolution places it among other politically debated, ethically trying, historically extrapolated, or purely philosophical propositions.

The National Wildlife Art Museum and U.S. Fish and Wildlife Interpretive Facility in Jackson Hole, Wyoming, metaphorically and literally reflects these social and cultural shifts, which demand new architectural types.

The ruined stone facade romantically proposes the marriage of the domesticated and the untamed and yields a subtle twist that goes well beyond the folly on the landscape to suggest a natural integration. Here shared-use design invites a new dialogue between teaching and exhibition. As in a melting pot, splitting and gathering of spaces cohesively define the functions of the facility. A fine arts museum performs within the context of a wildlife educational-interpretive facility and vice versa. The shared goal of education generated an interior hospitable to enlightenment.

Borders between interior and exterior are obfuscated to integrate building and landscape and reflect their consolidated purpose. Public areas permit viewing of the worlds venerated within the facility. Within these protected outdoor zones one can study natural terrain and landscapes as well as the behavior of multitudes of wildlife species protected within Yellowstone National Park and the National Elk Refuge.

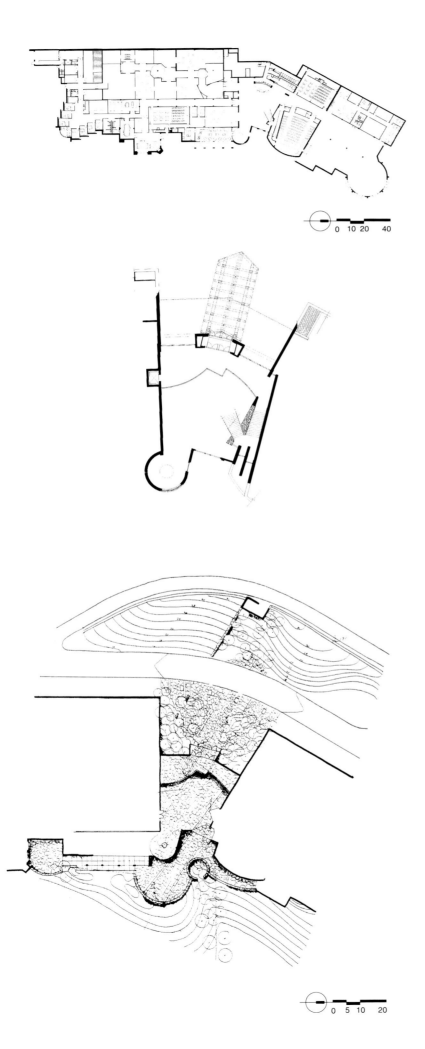

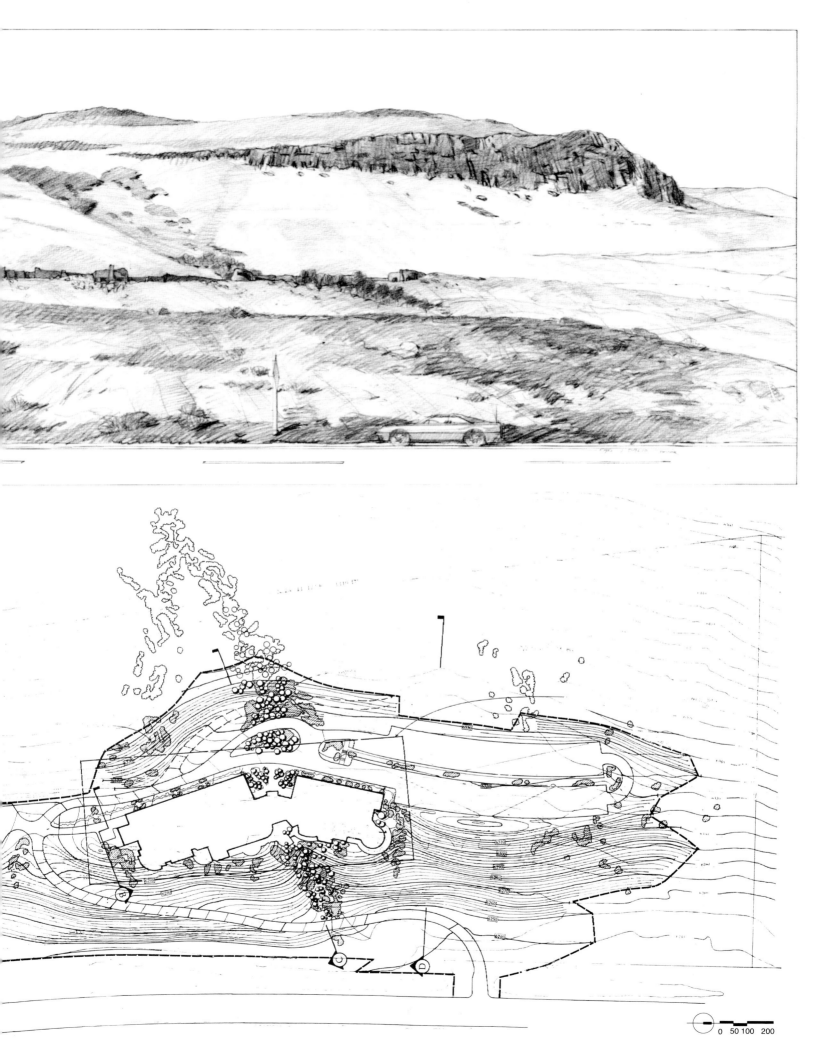

183

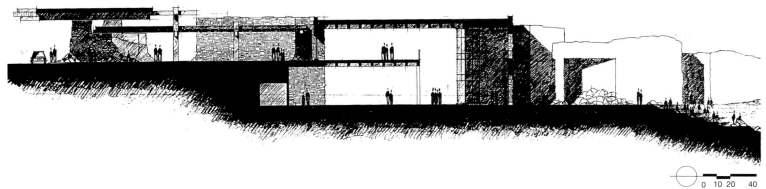

0 10 20   40

New Seoul International Airport

Seoul, Republic of South Korea

In keeping with Seoul's long-established identity as the "City of Contrasts," the New Seoul International Airport is a contemporary architectural impression married to the city's historical royal ambiance. As such, the design expresses ancient and modern culture, a totality respectfully forged from the shores of the Yellow Sea.

To this end, each element of the design was meticulously planned and engineered. A great hall in the main terminal organizes the facility by addressing pedestrian traffic-flow patterns. Each passenger, visitor, and employee passes through this memorable space. Throughout the facility, natural daylight and the interior landscaping of a Korean garden provide a more pleasant travel experience for each passenger.

The airport's subtle design uniquely showcases Korean culture and technology. The profile is inspired by historic Korean buildings but does not deliberately evoke traditional styles. The form of the concourse roof recalls ancient Korean palaces, but the masts and the catenary system supporting the roof evoke the large ships that sit at anchor adjacent to the new airport in Inchon Harbor.

This design clearly expresses Korea's natural ecological forms and contrasts them with the region's contemporary built environment. As such, the airport has the potential to evoke a lasting positive memory of Korea for the world's travelers passing through its gates. It thus provides a symbol clearly Korean in inspiration and execution.

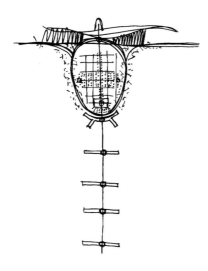

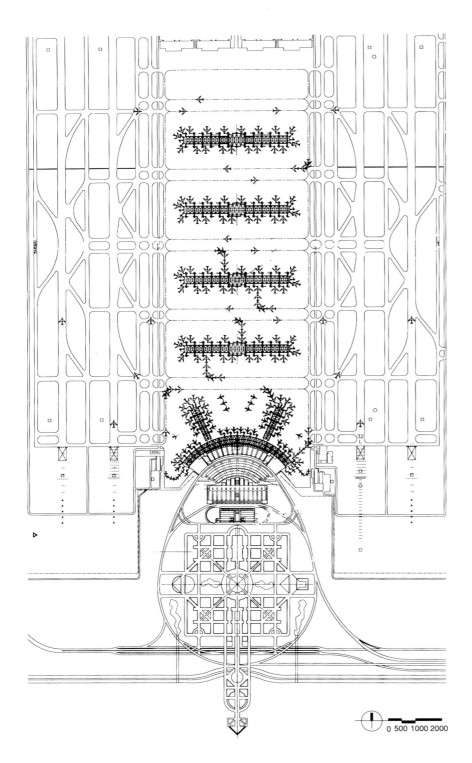

0 500 1000 2000

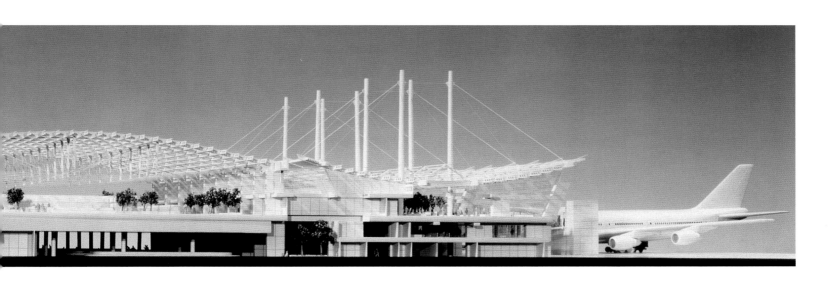

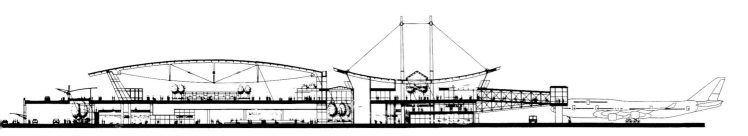

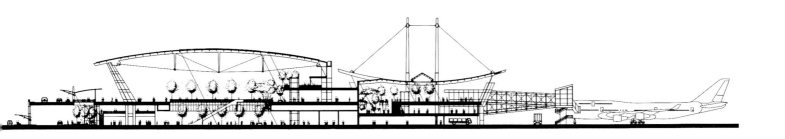

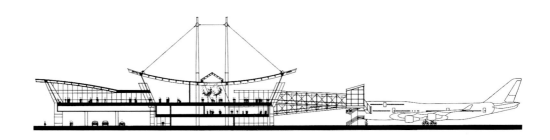

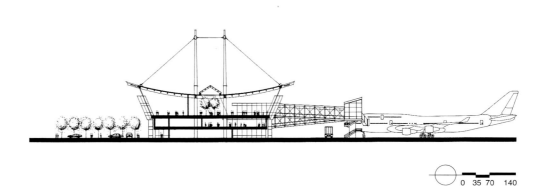

0 35 70 140

191

Second Bangkok International Airport

Bangkok, Thailand

The airport terminal, perhaps the most modern building type, is also the modern era's most paradoxical. Without a past, and in an era when conventional terms such as "history," "style," and "architecture" are being neutered by philosophical discourse, the airport, or more precisely the idea of the airport, has struggled to succeed. Antonio Sant'Elia's futurist conceptual drawings, *Citta' Nuova*, reveal the genesis of modern life, a place where transportation, including aircraft, is the most important aspect of the utopian city. Eero Saarinen's realizations of Sant'Elia's vision articulated the airport as architecture. No longer theory, this new building type as realized by Saarinen is a multicomplex urban mass under one common roof. Saarinen's approach, a large, open space well-scaled for circulation, with an emphatically realized, metaphorically rich roofline referencing the physiological principles and enabling anatomy of flight, appears in his designs for the TWA Terminal at John F. Kennedy International Airport in New York and the main terminal for Dulles International Airport outside Washington, D.C. This remains the literal and metaphorical paradigm of successful airport design.

The Fentress Bradburn design for the Second Bangkok International Airport reveals itself architecturally in much the same way. Large, distinctive circulation areas are crowned with a roof easily identified from both sky and earth. The poetry of an idea becomes a contemporary icon in the elegantly sculpted roof and the contextual details of the main building mass.

As airports become desired symbols of global economic strength, political and economic entities will demand transportation gateways of memorial and memorable quality that transcend existing examples. Fentress Bradburn here takes the opportunity to make a new, contextual mark.

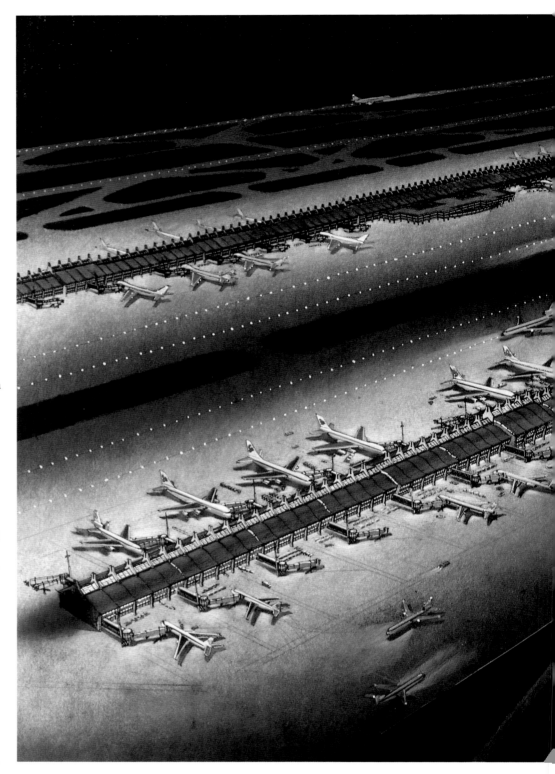

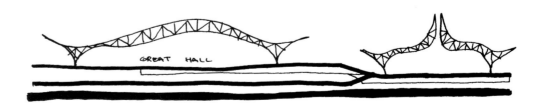

GREAT HALL

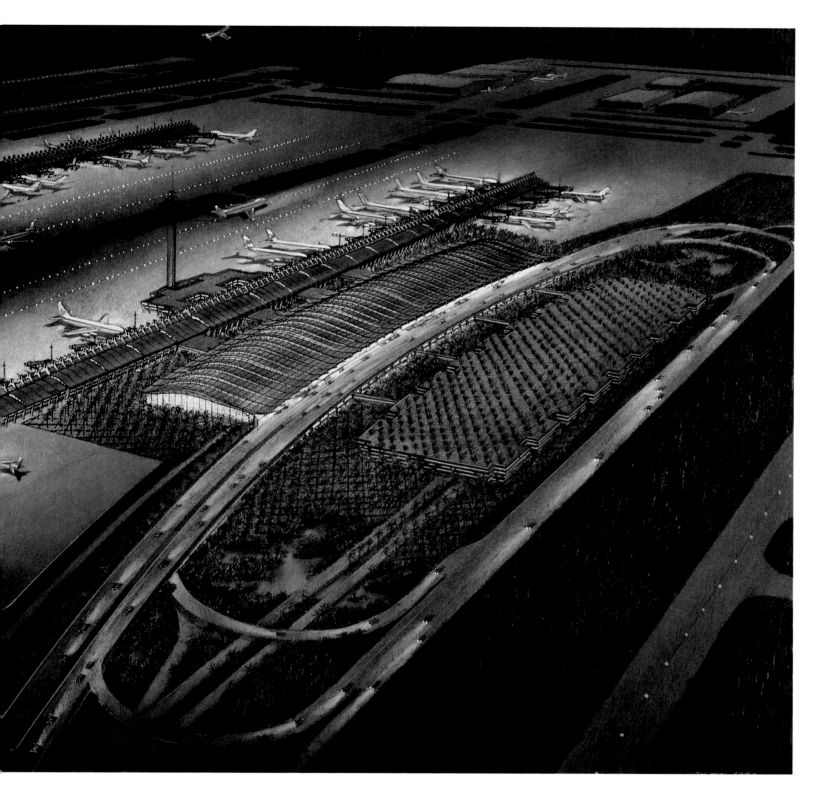

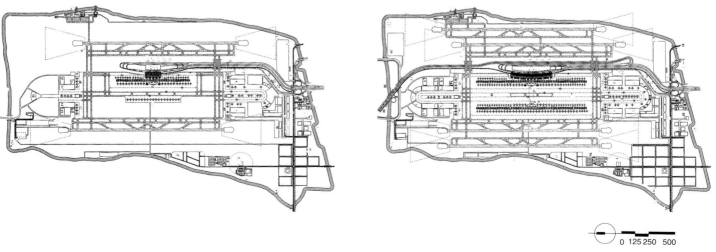

0 125 250 500

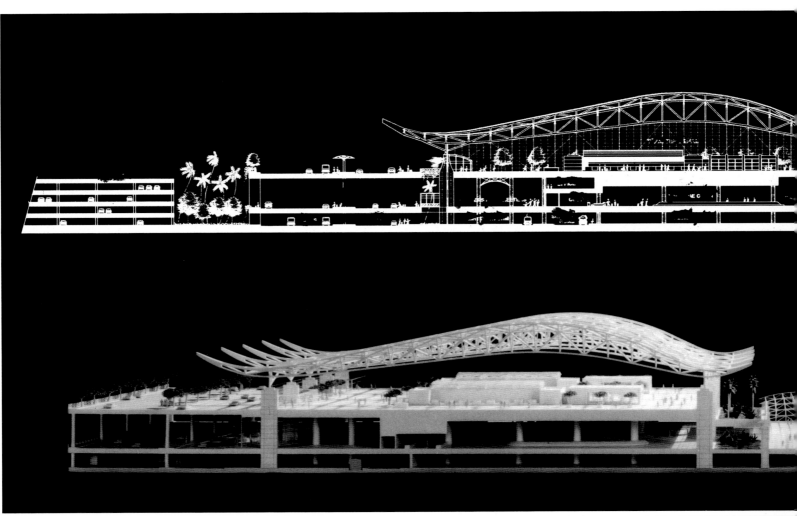

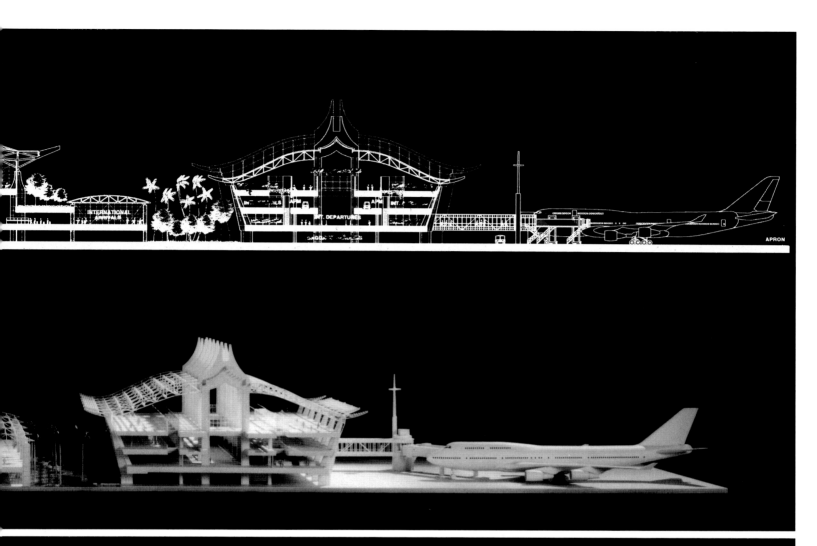

Souks of Beirut

Beirut, Lebanon

To revive Beirut, to reincarnate its heart and soul, is to restore the dynamic culture of its open markets, the souks. Foreign influences have long manipulated the character of this city, yet throughout a tumultuous past this magnificent urban complex has maintained its unique character. The souks will reestablish Beirut's identity, an image and a memory, honoring tradition, enhancing the interaction of merchant and customer, and reinforcing the sense of belonging. This revived district will entice visitors through the modern medium of busy night life and shopping. It will nurture the intimate relationship between man and nature along richly landscaped pathways and vibrant spaces animated with trickling water.

The reconstructed souks draw inspiration from the memory of the old and create a precedent for the future. With human scale, soft detailing, and inviting alleys, lanes, and squares, the new souks provide the foundation for a spiritual and soulful revival of the heart of Beirut. Architectural detailing allows for personal interaction between merchant and customer, tourist and resident, young and old. No specific style or material dominates the space, only the vibrancy of the shops and the energy of the crowds. This undemonstrative architecture affords each participant a personal response; this is the true intention behind the redesign. Traditional design, form, scale, and material in a modern application create an efficient marketplace that belies the complexities inherent in the life of Beirut.

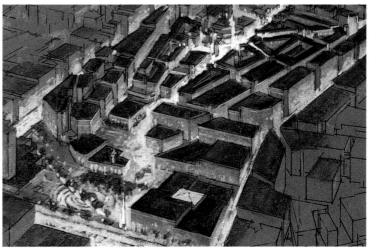

FIGURE GROUND
SCHEMATIC CONCEPT DIAGRAM

0 100 200 400

VEHICULAR CIRCULATION
SCHEMATIC CONCEPT DIAGRAM

■ at-grade circulation
- - - below grade circulation
•••• service access

PEDESTRIAN CIRCULATION
SCHEMATIC CONCEPT DIAGRAM

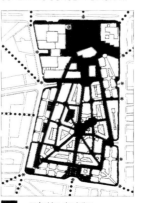

■ pedestrian circulation
•••• pedestrian connection to city
* gateway

MERCHANDISING PLAN

souks
retail and commercial mixed use
retail and residential mixed use

Dinosaur Discovery Museum

Canyon City, Colorado

Creating an identity for a center that celebrates old things found and the way they are discovered uncovered a methodology for the exploration of ecological expressionism. Constructing the signifier for the signified was accomplished by sculpturally identifying the structure as the partially exposed remains of some prehistoric creature. It spatially recalls a sculptural trellis, an architectural icon which invites the curious to experience what lies beyond.

The subtlety of the design exists in and on the earth where excavating for objects is translated into preserving the excavated spaces for occupation. Herein also lies the strength of the design, for a literal interpretation of structural requirements has evolved from an object that is seen as living or having once lived.

The excavations in the earth delineate circulation and define spaces for occupation. Significant is the way in which the idea of prefunction, circulation, and spatial relationships remained identifiable yet curious and subtle. Skylights serve as a visual connector while the spine as the ribs emerging from the earth's skin suggests a greater creature yet uncovered. These relationships imply that more excavation will occur. They express architecture which is additive, harmonious, and whole, yet revealed as if it has existed from ancient ages.

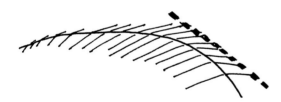

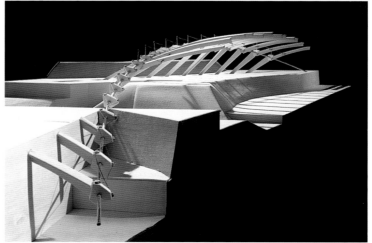

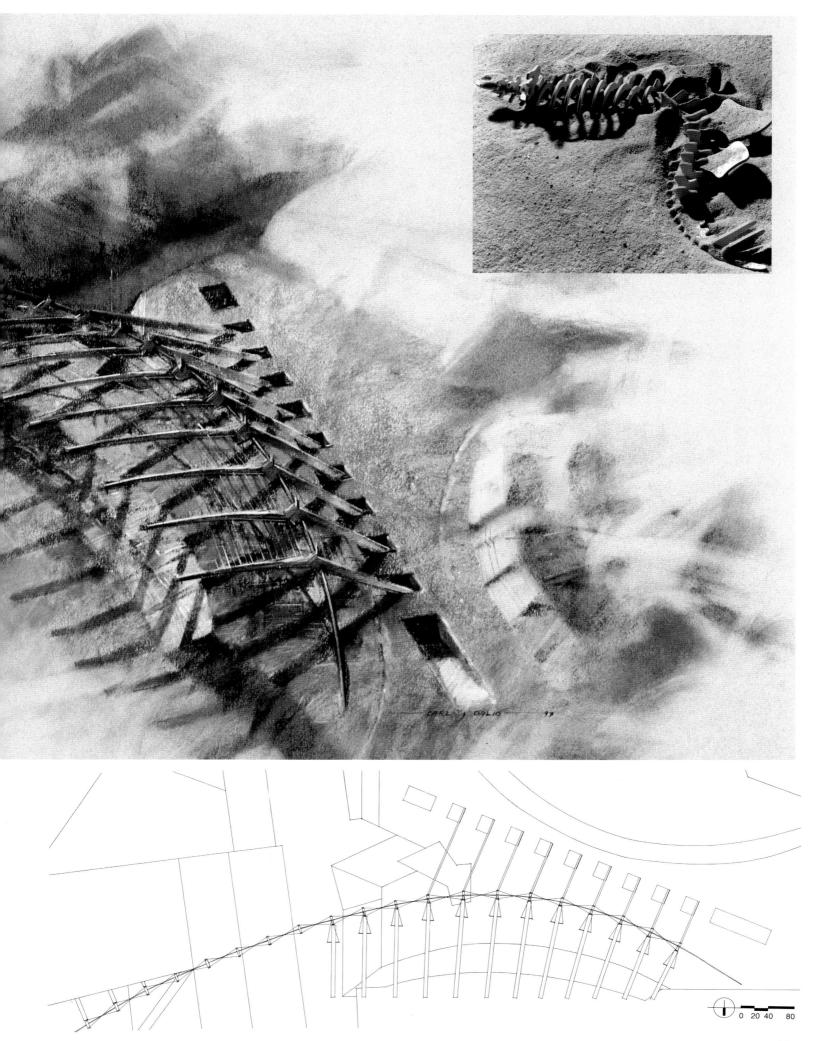

Crystal Center
Denver, Colorado, 1980

Chesman Realty Company

Principal-in-charge of design:
Curtis W. Fentress
Design team: Brian Chaffee, Lisa K. Fudge

Milestone Square Master Plan
Englewood, Colorado, 1981–86

J. Roulier Interests

Principal-in-charge of design:
Curtis W. Fentress
Principal-in-charge of production:
James H. Bradburn
Design team: Robert Busch, Brian Chaffee, Gregory R. Gidez, Stuart A. Schunck, Dave B. Weigand

Terrace Building
Englewood, Colorado, 1981

J. Roulier Interests

Principal-in-charge of design:
Curtis W. Fentress
Design team: Robert T. Brodie, Brian Chaffee, Mary Jane Donovan, Lisa K. Fudge, Frederic M. Harrington

Southbridge One
Littleton, Colorado, 1981

J. Roulier Interests

Principal-in-charge of design:
Curtis W. Fentress
Principal-in-charge of production:
James W. Bradburn
Design team: Robert Brodie, Lisa K. Fudge, Elizabeth Hamilton, Frederic M. Harrington, Robert J. O'Donnell

One Mile High Plaza
Denver, Colorado, 1981

J. Roulier Interests

Principal-in-charge of design:
Curtis W. Fentress
Design team: Brian Chaffee, Mary Jane Donovan, Lisa K. Fudge, Chris Weber

116 Inverness Drive East
Englewood, Colorado, 1982

Central Development Group

Principal-in-charge of design:
Curtis W. Fentress
Principal-in-charge of production:
James H. Bradburn
Design team: Gregory R. Gidez, James F. Hartman, Michael Kicklighter, Dan Naegele, James Niemi, Byron Stewart

Milestone Tower
Englewood, Colorado, 1982

J. Roulier Interests

Principal-in-charge of design:
Curtis W. Fentress
Principal-in-charge of production:
James H. Bradburn
Design team: Benjamin Berg,Donald W. DeCoster, Mary Jane Donovan, Robert C. Grubbs, John L. Mason

Kittredge Building
Denver, Colorado, 1982

Kittredge Properties

Principal-in-charge of design:
Curtis W. Fentress
Principal-in-charge of production:
James H. Bradburn
Design team: Deborah R. Allen, Brian Chaffee, Peter Frothingham, Gregory R. Gidez, Frederic M. Harrington, James F. Hartman, JoAnne Hege, Patrick M. McKelvey, Robert J. O'Donnell, John R. Taylor

Reliance Center
Denver, Colorado, 1982

Reliance Development

Principal-in-charge of design:
Curtis W. Fentress
Principal-in-charge of production:
James H. Bradburn
Design team: Robert T. Brodie, Brian Chaffee, Gary Chamers, Lisa K. Fudge, Gregory R. Gidez, JoAnne Hege, John K. McCauley, Patrick M. McKelvey, James Niemi, Michael O. Winters

Capitol Tower/J.D. Tower
Denver, Colorado, 1982

Dikeou Family Interest

Principal-in-charge of design:
Curtis W. Fentress
Design team: Gary Chamers

Odd Fellows Hall
Denver, Colorado, 1983

Cambridge Development Group

Principal-in-charge of design:
Curtis W. Fentress
Principal-in-charge of production:
James H. Bradburn
Design team: Deborah Allen, Frederic Harrington, James Hartman, JoAnne Hege, Leslie Leydorf, Carla McConnell, Patrick McKelvey, James Niemi, Nathaniel Taiwo, Dave Weigand, Richard Weldon, Toshika Yoshida

YMCA
Denver, Colorado, 1983

Jeffrey Selby & Jay Peterson, Associates

Principal-in-charge of design:
Curtis W. Fentress
Principal-in-charge of production:
James H. Bradburn
Design team: Gary Chamers

**Museum of Western Art/
The Navarre**
Denver, Colorado, 1983

William Foxley

Principal-in-charge of design:
Curtis W. Fentress
Principal-in-charge of production:
James H. Bradburn
Design team: Deborah R. Allen, Donald W. DeCoster, Douglas Dick
Associate architect: John Prosser

Englewood Mixed-use Center
Englewood, Colorado, 1984

Talley Corporation

Principal-in-charge of design:
Curtis W. Fentress
Principal-in-charge of production:
James H. Bradburn
Design team: B. Edward Balkin, Douglas Dick

Southbridge Plaza
Littleton, Colorado, 1984

Southbridge Plaza Association, Inc.

Principal-in-charge of design:
Curtis W. Fentress
Principal-in-charge of production:
James H. Bradburn
Design team: Elizabeth Hamilton, Kimble Hobbs, Bruce R. Mosteller, W. Harrison Phillips, Brit Probst, Bryon Stewart

Castlewood Plaza Master Plan
Englewood, Colorado, 1984

J. Roulier Interests

Principal-in-charge of design:
Curtis W. Fentress
Principal-in-charge of production:
James H. Bradburn
Design team: B. Edward Balkin, Steve Nelson

Tucson City Center Master Plan
Tucson, Arizona, 1984

Reliance Development Group

Principal-in-charge of design:
Curtis W. Fentress
Principal-in-charge of production:
James H. Bradburn
Project Designer: Michael Winters

Mountain Bell Special Services Center
Denver, Colorado, 1984

Mountain Bell

Principal-in-charge of design:
Curtis W. Fentress
Principal-in-charge of production:
James H. Bradburn
Design team: Deborah R. Allen, Donald W. DeCoster, Annette English, Gregory R. Gidez, Frank G. Hege, JoAnne Hege, James W. O'Neill, Frederick R. Pax, Toshika Yoshida

Balboa Company
Denver, Colorado, 1984

Frederick R. Meyer

Principal-in-charge of design:
Curtis W. Fentress
Principal-in-charge of production:
James H. Bradburn
Design team: Deborah R. Allen, Donald W. DeCoster, Gregory R. Gidez, JoAnne Hege, Stan Kulesa, James W. O'Neill, Toshika Yoshida

Pioneer Plaza Hotel
Denver, Colorado, 1984

Cambridge Development Group

Principal-in-charge of design:
Curtis W. Fentress
Principal-in-charge of production:
James H. Bradburn
Design team: Gary Chamers, Lisa K. Fudge, Gregory R. Gidez, Michael O. Winters

Greenville Park Tower
Dallas, Texas, 1984

JRI International/Robert Halloway Corporation

Principal-in-charge of design:
Curtis W. Fentress
Principal-in-charge of production:
James H. Bradburn
Project architect: Michael O. Winters
Design team: Garrett M. Christnacht, Steven O. Gregory, Clement Okoye, James W. O'Neill, John R. Taylor

Temple Sinai
Denver, Colorado, 1984

Temple Sinai Congregation

Principal-in-charge of design:
Curtis W. Fentress
Principal-in-charge of production:
James H. Bradburn
Project designer: B. Edward Balkin
Project manager: John K. McCauley
Design team: Ava Dahlstrom, Dalas Disney, John R. Taylor

1999 Broadway
Denver, Colorado, 1985

Lawder Corporation

Principal-in-charge of design:
Curtis W. Fentress
Principal-in-charge of production:
James H. Bradburn
Project designer: Michael O. Winters
Project manager: John K. McCauley
Job captain: Brit Probst
Design team: Robert T. Brodie, Robert G. Datson, Donald W. DeCoster, Lawrence Depenbusch, Douglas Dick, Gregory R. Gidez, Frederic M. Harrington, Michael Kicklighter, John M. Kudrycki, John L. Mason, Patrick M. McKelvey, James Niemi, Clement Okoye, Frederick R. Pax, Sandy Prouty, John R. Taylor, Mark A. Wagner, Toshika Yoshida

Holy Ghost Roman Catholic Church
Denver, Colorado, 1985

Lawder Corporation

Principal-in-charge of design:
Curtis W. Fentress
Principal-in-charge of production:
James H. Bradburn
Project architect: Michael O. Winters
Project manager: John L. Mason
Design team: Elizabeth Hamilton,
John M. Kudrycki, Patrick M.
McKelvey, Bruce R. Mosteller, John
R. Taylor

Welton Street Parking Garage
Denver, Colorado, 1985

Lawder Corporation

Principal-in-charge of design:
Curtis W. Fentress
Principal-in-charge of production:
James H. Bradburn
Project architect: Michael O. Winters
Project manager: John K. McCauley
Job captain: Patrick M. McKelvey
Design team: Douglas Dick, Frederic
M. Harrington, Kimble Hobbs, John
L. Mason, Brit Probst

1800 Grant Street
Denver, Colorado, 1985

1800 Grant Street Association, Ltd.

Principal-in-charge of design:
Curtis W. Fentress
Principal-in-charge of production:
James H. Bradburn
Project designer: Brian Chaffee
Project manager: John K. McCauley
Job captain: James F. Hartman
Design team: Deborah R. Allen,
Gregory R. Gidez, Renata Hajek,
JoAnne Hege, Mark A. Wagner,
Toshika Yoshida

Republic Park Hotel
Englewood, Colorado, 1985

Stan Miles Properties

Principal-in-charge of design:
Curtis W. Fentress
Principal-in-charge of production:
James H. Bradburn
Project manager: Mark A. Wagner
Interior designer: Victor Huff and
Associates
Design team: Lyle R. Anderson, Brian
Chaffee, Gary Chambers, John K.
McCauley

One DTC Tower
Englewood, Colorado, 1985

Corum Real Estate Interests

Principal-in-charge of design:
Curtis W. Fentress
Principal-in-charge of production:
James H. Bradburn
Project designer: B. Edward Balkin
Project manager: Dalas Disney
Design team: Deborah R. Allen, Lyle
R. Anderson, Garrett M. Christnacht,
Gregory R. Gidez, Renata Hajek,
Frederic M. Harrington, Stan Kulesa,
James Niemi, Clement Okoye, Brit
Probst, John R.Taylor, Toshika
Yoshida

Lexington Center
Colorado Springs, Colorado, 1985

Techkor Development

Principal-in-charge of design:
Curtis W. Fentress
Principal-in-charge of production:
James H. Bradburn
Project designer: Brian Chaffee
Project manager: John K. McCauley
Job captain: Patrick M. McKelvey

**Centennial Office Park
Master Plan**
Englewood, Colorado, 1985

Mission Viejo

Principal-in-charge of design:
Curtis W. Fentress
Principal-in-charge of production:
James H. Bradburn
Design team: B. Edward Balkin,
Charlotte C. Breed

Parkway Plaza Master Plan
Littleton, Colorado, 1985

Talley Corporation

Principal-in-charge of design:
Curtis W. Fentress
Principal-in-charge of production:
James H. Bradburn
Design team: Charlotte C. Breed

Fiddler's Green Ampitheater
Englewood, Colorado, 1985

John Madden Company

Principal-in-charge of design:
Curtis W. Fentress
Principal-in-charge of production:
James H. Bradburn
Design team: Galen Bailey, Todd R.
Britton, Amy Solomon

United Bank Tower
Tucson, Arizona, 1986

Reliance Development Group

Principal-in-charge of design:
Curtis W. Fentress
Principal-in-charge of production:
James H. Bradburn
Design team: Jane Bertschinger, Brian
Chaffee, Garrett Christnacht, Donald
DeCoster, Douglas Dick, Gregory Gi-
dez, Renata Hajek, Frank Hege, Stan Ku-
lesa, John Mason, James Niemi, James
O'Neill, Jim Snyder, Michael O. Winters

Terrace Tower II
Englewood, Colorado, 1986

J. Roulier Interests
First Texas Savings Association

Principal-in-charge of design:
Curtis W. Fentress
Principal-in-charge of production:
James H. Bradburn
Project designer: Donald W. DeCoster
Design team: Deborah R. Allen, Frank
G. Hege, John M. Kudrycki, James
Niemi, Frederick R. Pax, Brit Probst

**Data General Field Engineering
Logistics Center**
Fountain, Colorado, 1986

Data General Corporation

Principal-in-charge of design:
Curtis W. Fentress
Principal-in-charge of production:
James H. Bradburn
Project designer: B. Edward Balkin
Project manager: Brit Probst
Job captain: John M. Kudrycki
Design team: Garrett M. Christnacht,
Frank G. Hege, Renata Hajek, Steven
Fritzky

Black American West Museum
Denver, Colorado, 1987

Black American West Museum

Principal-in-charge of design:
Curtis W. Fentress
Principal-in-charge of production:
James H. Bradburn
Project architect: James F. Hartman
Design team: Mark Brinkman, Donald
W. DeCoster, Mary Jane Koenig,
Francis Mishler

Sun Plaza
Colorado Springs, Colorado, 1987

Sun Resources, Inc.

Principal-in-charge of design:
Curtis W. Fentress
Principal-in-charge of production:
James H. Bradburn
Project designer: Luis O. Acosta
Project manager: John K. McCauley
Job captain: Patrick M. McKelvey
Design team: Sandy Brand, Gregory
R. Gidez, Frederick R. Pax, John R.
Taylor

Boise Civic Center
Boise, Idaho, 1987

Dick Holtz

Principal-in-charge of design:
Curtis W. Fentress
Principal-in-charge of production:
James H. Bradburn
Project architect: Michael O. Winters

Oxbridge Town Center
Oxbridge, England, 1988

David Sparrow

Principal-in-charge of design:
Curtis W. Fentress
Principal-in-charge of production:
James H. Bradburn
Project designer: Michael O. Winters
Design team: Douglas Dick

Denver Permit Center
Denver, Colorado, 1989

City and County of Denver,
Colorado

Principal-in-charge of design:
Curtis W. Fentress
Principal-in-charge of production:
James H. Bradburn
Project manager: James F. Hartman
Design team: James Carpenter, Robert
G. Datson, Philip Davis, Beverly G.
Pax, Frederick R. Pax, Robert Root,
John M. Salisbury, Les Stuart

Western and American Galleries,
Denver Art Museum
Denver, Colorado, 1989

Denver Art Museum

Principal-in-charge of design:
Curtis W. Fentress
Principal-in-charge of production:
James H. Bradburn
Design team: Robert Root, Michael
Gengler, John M. Salisbury

Idaho Power Company
Corporate Headquarters
Boise, Idaho, 1989

Idaho Power Company

Principal-in-charge of design:
Curtis W. Fentress
Principal-in-charge of production:
James H. Bradburn
Architect-of-record: CSHQA Architects
and Planners
Project architect: Michael O. Winters
Space planning: Sandy Prouty
Design team: Robert G. Datson, Karin
Mason, Jack Mousseau, Jun Xia

Franklin and Lake
Chicago, Illinois, 1989

Zeller Realty

Principal-in-charge of design:
Curtis W. Fentress
Principal-in-charge of production:
James H. Bradburn
Project architect: Michael O. Winters
Design team: Jun Xia

Jefferson County Government
Center Master Plan
Golden, Colorado, 1989–92

Jefferson County, Colorado

Principal-in-charge of design:
Curtis W. Fentress
Principal-in-charge of production:
James H. Bradburn
Project architect: B. Edward Balkin
Design team: Brian Chaffee

Jefferson County Human Services
Building
Golden, Colorado, 1989

Jefferson County, Colorado

Principal-in-charge of design:
Curtis W. Fentress
Principal-in-charge of production:
James H. Bradburn
Design team: B. Edward Balkin,
Renata Hajek, Barbara K.
Hochstetler, John M. Kudrycki, John
L. Mason, Mark A. Wagner

Colorado State Capitol
Life-Safety Project
Denver, Colorado, 1989–99

State of Colorado

Principal-in-charge of design:
Curtis W. Fentress
Principal-in-charge of production:
James H. Bradburn
Project architect: James F. Hartman
Design team: Garrett M. Christnacht,
Ala F. Hason, Brian Ostler, John M.
Salisbury, Samuel Tyner

Colorado Convention Center
Denver, Colorado, 1990

City and County of Denver,
Colorado

Principal-in-charge of design:
Curtis W. Fentress
Principal-in-charge of production:
James H. Bradburn
Project designer: Michael O. Winters
Project manager: Brit Probst
Interior designer: Barbara K.
Hochstetler
Design team: B. Edward Balkin,
Richard Burkett, Brian Chaffee,
Melanie Colcord, Gregory R. Gidez,
Nancy Kettner, John M. Kudrycki,
Lauren Lee, Greg Lemon, Beverly G.
Pax, John M. Salisbury, Les Stuart,
Mark A. Wagner
Associate architects: Loschky
MarQuardt and Nesholm;
Bertram A. Bruton and Associates

IBM Customer Briefing Center
Boulder, Colorado, 1990

IBM

Principal-in-charge of design:
Curtis W. Fentress
Principal-in-charge of production:
James H. Bradburn
Project designer: Barbara K. Hochstetler
Project manager: Donald W. DeCoster
Design team: Robert G. Datson,
Kathleen Corner Galvin, John A.
Gossett, Judith Jump, Sandy Prouty,
Michael O. Winters

**Colorado School of Mines
Engineering Hall Renovation**
Golden, Colorado, 1990

Colorado School of Mines

Principal-in-charge of design:
Curtis W. Fentress
Principal-in-charge of production:
James H. Bradburn
Design team: Robert G. Datson, James
F. Hartman, Nancy Kettner, Ned
Kirschbaum, Robert Root, Robert
Young

Cherry Creek Plaza
Denver, Colorado, 1988–90

Bramalea

Principal-in-charge of design:
Curtis W. Fentress
Principal-in-charge of production:
James H. Bradburn
Design team: B. Edward Balkin

Westlake Residences
Seattle, Washington, 1990

Astral Investments

Principal-in-charge of design:
Curtis W. Fentress
Principal-in-charge of production:
James H. Bradburn
Project architect: Christopher A.
Carvell
Project manager: Mark A. Wagner
Design team: Richard Burkett, Peter
D. Carlson

809 Olive Way
Seattle, Washington, 1990

Western Securities Ltd.

Principal-in-charge of design:
Curtis W. Fentress
Principal-in-charge of production:
James H. Bradburn
Project architect: Christopher A.
Carvell
Project manager: Mark A. Wagner
Design team: Ronald R. Booth, Robert
Louden

**Denver Central Library
Urban Analysis**
Denver, Colorado, 1990

City and County of Denver,
Colorado

Principal-in-charge of design:
Curtis W. Fentress
Principal-in-charge of production:
James H. Bradburn
Design team: Arthur A. Hoy, III,
Michel Pariseau

Union Station Redevelopment Plan
Denver, Colorado, 1990–91

Union Station Redevelopment
Committee

Principal-in-charge of design:
Curtis W. Fentress
Principal-in-charge of production:
James H. Bradburn
*Design team:*Galen Bailey, III, Todd
Britton, Arthur A. Hoy

Ronstadt Transit Center
Tucson, Arizona, 1991

City of Tucson, Arizona

Principal-in-charge of design:
Curtis W. Fentress
Principal-in-charge of production:
James H. Bradburn
Project designer: Brian Chaffee
Project manager: Robert Louden,
Design team: James Carpenter, John L.
Mason, Clement Okoye, Robert Root,
Michael O. Winters

Cathedral Square
Milwaukee, Wisconsin, 1991

Corum Real Estate Group

Principal-in-charge of design:
Curtis W. Fentress
Principal-in-charge of production:
James H. Bradburn
Design team: Peter D. Carlson

**Denver International Airport,
Passenger Terminal Complex**
Denver, Colorado, 1991–94

City and County of Denver,
Colorado

Principal-in-charge of design:
Curtis W. Fentress
Principal-in-charge of production:
James H. Bradburn
Project architect: Michael O. Winters
Project director: Thomas J. Walsh
Interior designer: Barbara K.
Hochstetler
Project manager: Brit Probst
Job captains: Joseph Solomon, John M.
Salisbury
Design team: Galen Bailey, Todd R.
Britton, Richard Burkett, James
Carney, James Carpenter, Brian
Chaffee, Garrett M. Christnacht, John
Gagnon, Kathleen Corner Galvin,
Michael Gengler, Gregory R. Gidez,
Warren Hogue, III, Doris Hung,
Charles Johns, Anthia Kappos,
Michael Klebba, John M. Kudrycki,
Lauren Lee, Robert Louden, Michael
Miller, Gary Morris, Jack M.
Mousseau, A. Chris Olson, Brian
Ostler, Teri Paris, Frederick R. Pax,
Robert Root, Tim Roush, Amy
Solomon, Les Stuart, Dave Tompkins,
Samuel Tyner, Mark A. Wagner, John
C. Wurzenberger, Jr., Jun Xia
Associate architects: Pouw and
Associates, Inc.,
Bertram A. Bruton and Associates

University Art Museum
University of California at Santa
Barbara
Santa Barbara, California, 1991

University of California at Santa
Barbara

Principal-in-charge of design:
Curtis W. Fentress
Principal-in-charge of production:
James H. Bradburn
Project architect: Michael O. Winters
Design team: Douglas Dick
Associate architect: John Prosser

**Gemmill Mathematics Library and
Engineering Sciences Building**
Boulder, Colorado, 1992

University of Colorado at Boulder

Principal-in-charge of design:
Curtis W. Fentress
Principal-in-charge of production:
James H. Bradburn
Project designer: Christopher A.
Carvell
Design team: Robert Louden, Gary
Morris, Nancy Kettner, Douglas
Eichelberger, Greg Lemon, Robert
Root, Michael O. Winters, Jun Xia

Jefferson County Courts and Administration Building
Golden, Colorado, 1992

Jefferson County, Colorado

Principal-in-charge of design:
Curtis W. Fentress
Principal-in-charge of production:
James H. Bradburn
Project designer: Brian Chaffee
Project manager: James F. Hartman
Interior designer: Barbara K.
Hochstetler
Design team: Gregory D. Billingham,
Bill Bramblett, Sandy J. Brand,
Richard Burkett, James Carney,
James Carpenter, Douglas
Eichelberger, Gregory R. Gidez, Ala
F. Hason, Judith Jump, Ned
Kirschbaum, Lauren Lee, Robert
Louden, John L. Mason, Clement
Okoye, Beverly G. Pax, Brit Probst,
Samuel Tyner, Mark A. Wagner, Lynn
Wisecarver Johnson

Natural Resources Building
Olympia, Washington, 1992

Department of General
Administration
East Campus Plus Program
State of Washington

Principal-in-charge of design:
Curtis W. Fentress
Principal-in-charge of production:
James H. Bradburn
Project architect: Ronald R. Booth
Interior designer: Barbara K.
Hochstetler
Project manager: John M. Kudrycki
Job captain: Gregory R. Gidez
Design team: James Carney, Milan
Hart, Arthur A. Hoy, III, Lynn
Wisecarver Johnson, Lauren Lee,
David Tompkins, Michael Wisneski

New Seoul International Airport Passenger Terminal Complex
Seoul, Korea, 1992

City of Seoul, Korea

Principal-in-charge of design:
Curtis W. Fentress
Principal-in-charge of production:
James H. Bradburn
Project architect: Jack M. Mousseau
Interior designer: Barbara K.
Hochstetler
Project director: Thomas J. Walsh
Job captain: Richard Burkett
Design team: Galen Bailey, Todd R.
Britton, Richard Burkett, John
Gagnon, Arthur A. Hoy, III, Anthia
Kappos, Ned Kirschbaum, Lauren
Lee, John M. McGahey, Wilbur
Moore, Gary Morris, Brian Ostler,
Michelle Ray, Tim Roush, Amy
Solomon, Les Stuart, Michael O.
Winters, John C. Wurzenberger, Jr.
Associate architects: Baum, Hi-Lim,
Jung-Lim, Wodushi Architects (BHJW);
McClier Aviation Group

Dinosaur Discovery Museum
Canyon City, Colorado, 1992

Garden Park Paleontological Society

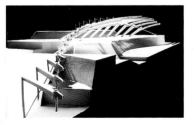

Principal-in-charge of design:
Curtis W. Fentress
Principal-in-charge of production:
James H. Bradburn
Project architect: Brian Chaffee
Design Team: Carl J. Dalio, Wilbur
Moore

West Hills Hotel
Keystone, Colorado, 1992

Chamer Development

Principal-in-charge of design:
Curtis W. Fentress
Principal-in-charge of production:
James H. Bradburn
Project architect: Michael O. Winters
Project manager: Brit Probst
Design team: Gary Chamers, Mark A.
Wagner

Eastbank Conference Center and Hotel
Wichita, Kansas, 1992

Ross Investment

Principal-in-charge of design:
Curtis W. Fentress
Principal-in-charge of production:
James H. Bradburn
Project architect: Mark A. Wagner
Interior designer: Barbara K. Hochstetler

Colorado Convention Center Hotel
Denver, Colorado, 1992

J. Roulier Interests

Principal-in-charge of design:
Curtis W. Fentress
Principal-in-charge of production:
James H. Bradburn
Design team: Galen Bailey, Todd Britton, Amy Solomon, Jun Xia

Coors Stadium
Denver, Colorado, 1992

Denver Metropolitan Major League Baseball Stadium District Commission

Principal-in-charge of design:
Curtis W. Fentress
Principal-in-charge of production:
James H. Bradburn
Design team: John A. Gossett, Michael Pariseau
Associate architect; Ellerbe Becket Inc.

Kuala Lumpur Airport
Kuala Lumpur, 1992

McClier Aviation Group

Principal-in-charge of design:
Curtis W. Fentress
Principal-in-charge of production:
James H. Bradburn
Design team: Carl J. Dalio, Michael O. Winters

Moscow Redevelopment Project
Moscow, Russia, 1992

Moscow Redevelopment Group

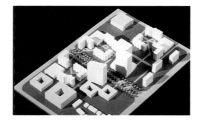

Principal-in-charge of design:
Curtis W. Fentress
Principal-in-charge of production:
James H. Bradburn
Design team: Arthur A. Hoy, III, Jack M. Mousseau, Aleksandr Sheykhet, Michael O. Winters
Associate architects: Andrei Meerson & Partners

Ogden-Weber State University Conference and Performing Arts Complex
Ogden, Utah, 1992

Weber County, Utah

Principal-in-charge of design:
Curtis W. Fentress
Principal-in-charge of production:
James H. Bradburn
Architect-of-record: Sanders Herman Associates
Project designer: Ronald R. Booth
Project architect: Christopher A. Carvell
Project manager: Mark A. Wagner
Design team: Gregory D. Billingham, Peter D. Carlson, Robert Herman, Michael Sanders, Thomas P. Theobald

Catalina Resort Community Plan
Playa Dantita, Ocotal,
Costa Rica, 1992

Developments International, Inc.

Principal-in-charge of design:
Curtis W. Fentress
Principal-in-charge of production:
James H. Bradburn
Project designer: Jack M. Mousseau
Project manager: Barbara K. Hochstetler
Design team: Wilbur Moore

Clark County Government Center
Las Vegas, Nevada, 1992

Clark County, Nevada

Principal-in-charge of design:
Curtis W. Fentress
Principal-in-charge of production:
James H. Bradburn
Project architect: Michael O. Winters
Interior designer: Barbara K.
Hochstetler
Project manager: John M. Kudrycki
Job captain: Ned Kirschbaum
Design team: Ronald R. Booth, John
A. Gossett, Ala F. Hason, Warren
Hogue, III, Arthur A. Hoy, III, Anthia
Kappos, Lauren Lee, Robert Louden,
Gary Morris, Joy Spatz, Michael
Wisneski, John C. Wurzenberger, Jr.
Associate architect: Domingo
Cambeiro Corporation

National Cowboy Hall of Fame
Oklahoma City, Oklahoma, 1992

National Cowboy Hall of Fame and
Western Heritage Center

Principal-in-charge of design:
Curtis W. Fentress
Principal-in-charge of production:
James H. Bradburn
Project architect: Ronald R. Booth
Interior designer: Barbara K.
Hochstetler
Project manager: Mark A. Wagner
Job captain: Gregory D. Billingham
Design team: Peter D. Carlson, John
Gagnon, John M. McGahey, Gary
Morris, Jack M. Mousseau, Teri Paris,
Thomas P. Theobald

National Oceanic and Atmospheric
Administration Headquarters
Boulder, Colorado, 1992

United States General Services
Administration
National Oceanic and Atmospheric
Administration

Principal-in-charge of design:
Curtis W. Fentress
Principal-in-charge of production:
James H. Bradburn
Project architect: Ronald R. Booth
Interior designer: Barbara K.
Hochstetler
Project manager: Jeff Olson
Design team: Peter D. Carlson, Gregory
R. Gidez, Ala Hason, Warren Hogue, III,
Robert Louden, Gary Morris, Teri Paris

Estes Park Convention Center
Estes Park, Colorado, 1992

City of Estes Park, Colorado

Principal-in-charge of design:
Curtis W. Fentress
Principal-in-charge of production:
James H. Bradburn
Architect-of-record: Thorpe and Assoc.
Principal-in-charge: Roger Thorpe
Project architect: Christopher Carvell
Project manager: Mark A. Wagner
Interior designer: Barbara K.
Hochstetler

National Museum of Wildlife Art
Jackson, Wyoming, 1993

National Wildlife Art Museum
Bill and Joffa Kerr

Principal-in-charge of design:
Curtis W. Fentress
Principal-in-charge of production:
James H. Bradburn
Project architect: Brian Chaffee
Interior designer: Gary Morris
Job captain: Gregory R. Gidez
Design team: Anthia Kappos, Brian
Ostler, Tim Roush

Vladivostok City Center
Vladivostok, Russia, 1993

Jupiter Development

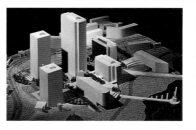

Principal-in-charge of design:
Curtis W. Fentress
Principal-in-charge of production:
James H. Bradburn
Project architect: Arthur A. Hoy, III
Design team: Doni Mitchell,
Aleksandr Sheykhet

Second Bangkok International Airport
Bangkok, Thailand, 1993

Airport Authority of Thailand

Principal-in-charge of design:
Curtis W. Fentress
Principal-in-charge of production:
James H. Bradburn
Project designer: Michael O. Winters
Interior designer: Barbara K. Hochstetler
Project architect: Jack M. Mousseau
Project manager: Thomas J. Walsh
Design team: Galen Bailey, Nina Bazian, Todd R. Britton, Catherine Dunn, David Goorman, John A. Gossett, John M. McGahey, Doni Mitchell, Gary Morris, Minh Nguyen, Brian Ostler, Amy Solomon, Voraporn Sundarupura
Associate architect: McClier Aviation Group

Kwangju Bank Headquarters
Kwangju, Korea, 1993

Kwangju Bank

Principal-in-charge of design:
Curtis W. Fentress
Principal-in-charge of production:
James H. Bradburn
Design team: Arthur A. Hoy, III

Hawaii Convention Center
Honolulu, Hawaii, 1994

State of Hawaii

Principal-in-charge of design:
Curtis W. Fentress
Principal-in-charge of production:
James H. Bradburn
Project architect: Michael O. Winters
Project manager: John M. Kudrycki
Project designer: Jack M. Mousseau
Interior designer: Gary Morris
Design team: Nina Bazian, Cydney Fisher, Michael Gengler, Haia Ghalib, John A. Gossett, Ala F. Hason, John M. McGahey, Michael Miller, Minh Nguyen, Aleksandr Sheykhet, Voraporn Sundarupura, Thomas J. Walsh, John C. Wurzenburger, Jr.
Associate architects: DMJM Hawaii; Kauahikaua and Chun Architects

Montrose Government Center
Montrose, Colorado, 1994

Montrose County, Colorado

Principal-in-charge of design:
Curtis W. Fentress
Principal-in-charge of production:
James H. Bradburn
Project architect: Christopher A. Carvell
Project designer: Brian Chaffee
Design team: Doni Mitchell, Aleksandr Sheykhet
Associate architect: Reilly Johnson, Architects

The Reconstruction of the Souks of Beirut: An International Ideas Competition
Beirut, Lebanon, 1994

Solidere

Principal-in-charge of design:
Curtis W. Fentress
Principal-in-charge of production:
James H. Bradburn
Project manager: Michael Wisneski
Project architect: Ala F. Hason
Architectural historian: Dr. Roger A. Chandler
Researcher: Mark T. Harpe
Design team: Nina Bazian, Jamili Butros Copty, Jack M. Mousseau, Minh Nguyen, Voraporn Sundarupura

Curtis Worth Fentress, AIA, RIBA
Principal-in-Charge of Design

Curtis W. Fentress was born in Greensboro, North Carolina, in 1947. He received a Bachelor of Architecture degree in 1972 from North Carolina State University, School of Design, where he finished at the top of his class. While still a student he was awarded an AIA-AIAF Fellowship (1970), a Graham Foundation Fellowship (1971), and the Alpha Rho Chi Medal, the highest honor bestowed on a designer by an American architectural school (1972).

After graduation Fentress joined the New York firm of I. M. Pei and Partners, where between 1972 and 1977 he worked on several international projects including the Raffles Place Center in Singapore. As a project designer for Kohn Pederson Fox of New York from 1977 to 1980, Fentress was responsible for designing the Amoco Building in Denver, Colorado, for which he received *Building Design and Construction* magazine's Young Professional of the Year award in 1977. In January 1980 Fentress formed C.W. Fentress and Associates.

C.W. Fentress J.H. Bradburn and Associates, P.C. (as the firm was renamed in 1990) is now the largest architectural firm in Colorado and employs more than seventy people. The practice has projects underway in more than a dozen states, the United Kingdom, the Commonwealth of Independent States, Central America, and the Republic of Korea. The firm has received some ninety-eight design awards, including thirty-four from the American Institute of Architects, since 1980.

As principal-in-charge of design, Fentress has directed the design of various large-scale projects including the Passenger Terminal Complex of the new Denver International Airport, the Colorado Convention Center, 1999 Broadway, One DTC, and the Jefferson County Government Center.

Fentress's projects also include prize-winning national competitions for the National Wildlife Art Museum in Jackson Hole, Wyoming; the Clark County Government Center in Las Vegas, Nevada; the Natural Resources Building in Olympia, Washington; and the National Cowboy Hall of Fame in Oklahoma City, Oklahoma. Most recently the firm won the international design competition for the New Seoul Metropolitan Airport in Seoul, Korea.

Fentress's work has been cited in *Retrospective of Courthouse Design: 1980–1991* (Williamsburg, Va.: National Center for State Courts, 1992) and *American Architecture: The State of the Art in the 80's* (Ashland, Ky.: Hanover Publishing Company, 1985).

Fentress was 1993 president of the Colorado Chapter of the American Institute of Architects. As a member of the Royal Institute of British Architects, the American Institute of Architects National Design Committee, the Urban Land Institute, the Urban Design Forum, and the Denver Chamber of Commerce and as a devotee of the keen young architectural mind, Fentress lectures widely and serves as visiting critic at colleges and universities across the United States.

James Henry Bradburn, AIA
Principal-in-Charge of Production

James H. Bradburn was born in Rochester, New York, in 1944. He received a Bachelor of Building Science in 1966 and a Bachelor of Architecture in 1967, both from Rensselaer Polytechnic Institute, where he also earned distinction as an athlete-scholar.

Prior to forming C.W. Fentress J.H. Bradburn and Associates, Bradburn was a designer with Vincent G. Kling and Associates from 1967 to 1968 and a project architect with Kevin Roche John Dinkeloo and Associates from 1968 to 1980.

Bradburn has practiced architecture since 1967. He is a member of the American Institute of Architects, the National Council of Architectural Registration Boards, the American Arbitration Association, the Construction Specifications Institute, the American Concrete Institute, and the American Society for Testing and Materials.

An architect with the heart of an engineer, Bradburn constantly seeks the highest levels of performance in production and architectural technology by applying sound engineering and science to the latest innovations in contemporary architecture. He has won many awards for technical achievement from both the architectural and engineering communities.

Bradburn's sensitivity to teamwork and constructive cooperation on multifaceted design projects has led him to advocate partnership building. He has lectured regionally on project partnering and team building. He has also published several significant articles on technology, including "New Attachment Technique: Alternative to Traditional Stone Cladding Systems," which appeared in *Modern Steel Construction* in 1981. Bradburn also applied one of the first four-sided, structural-silicone, insulated-glass curtain walls and the largest structurally integrated tensile-fabric roof in the world.

Bradburn balances professional activity with community service through involvement in the Rotary Club, the Denver Business Association, and the board of directors for the Colorado Christian Home (a treatment center for abused and neglected children and their families).

ASSOCIATES

Ronald R. Booth, AIA
Associate Principal
Bachelor of Architecture, 1973,
University of Kansas

Christopher A. Carvell, AIA
Associate Principal
Bachelor of Architecture, l974,
University of Kentucky

Barbara K. Hochstetler, ASID
Associate Principal
Bachelor of Fine Art, 1976,
California State University at Sacramento
Master of Fine Art in Interior Design, 1982
Colorado State University

Michael O. Winters, AIA
Associate Principal
Bachelor of Science in Architecture, 1977,
University of Wisconsin at Milwaukee;
Master of Architecture, 1980,
University of Colorado at Denver

James F. Hartman, AIA
Senior Associate
Bachelor of Science in Architecture, 1980,
University of Virginia

John M. Kudrycki, AIA
Senior Associate
Bachelor of Architecture, 1977,
Lawrence Institute of Technology

Thomas J. Walsh, AIA
Senior Associate
Bachelor of Architecture, 1973,
Oklahoma State University

Todd Rockwell Britton
Associate
College of Business and Administration,
University of Colorado at Boulder;
College of Liberal Arts and Sciences,
University of Colorado at Denver

Brian Chaffee, AIA
Associate
Bachelor of Architecture, 1981,
School of Architecture,
Montana State University

Arthur Andrew Hoy III, AIA
Associate
Bachelor of Science in Design, 1986,
Master of Architecture, 1988,
Arizona State University

Jack M. Mousseau, AIA
Associate
Bachelor of Architecture, 1985,
University of Idaho, Moscow

Mark A. Wagner
Associate
Bachelor of Architecture, 1969,
University of New Mexico;
Master of Architecture in Urban Design, 1972,
University of California at Berkeley

PROJECT ASSISTANTS

The following people have worked in the office of C.W Fentress J.H. Bradburn and Associates, P.C. between 1980 and 1994 and have contributed to the success of the projects presented in this volume.

Ana Acosta
Luis O. Acosta
Don Adams
Mary Adkins
Deborah R. Allen
Lyle R. Anderson
Jacqueline Y. April
Judy Arkulari
David Arnoth
Debbie Atencio
LeAlta Ayers
Galen Bailey
Antoinette Colonel Baines
Mary Baird
B. Edward Balkin
Linda I. Barclay
Melissa Bare
Margorie Bates
Karen Bauman
Nina Bazian
Nina Beardsley
Karen R. Beasley
Brian Beckler
Benjamin Berg
Jane Bertschinger
Gregory Biggs
Gregory D. Billingham
Susan Blosten
Blake Booth
Ronald R. Booth
James M. Boucher
Betty Lou Bowers
Barbara Bowman
James Henry Bradburn
Bill Bramblett
Sandy Brand
Daniel Braun
Charlotte C. Breed
Mark Brinkman
Todd R. Britton
Rosanne Brock
Robert T. Brodie
Andrew Bromberg
Russell Brown
Kristine Brundige
Carla Brunstead
Elizabeth Buckman
Richard Burkett
Robert Busch
David Caldwell
Katharine Capra
Peter D. Carlson
James Carney
James Carpenter
Carol A. Carr
Christopher A. Carvell
Brian Chaffee
Gary Chamers

Roger A. Chandler
Marilynn Charles
Deborah Chelemes
Garrett M. Christnacht
Arpie Christianian
    Chucovich
Andrew Clements
Roslyn Clinton
Jayne Coburn
Melanie Colcord
Martin Cole
Jacqueline Collard
Melora Collette
Pamela Combs
Sonia Rocio Contreras
Cheryl Cooper
Vicky Cooper
Ruth Cramer
Delores Cuba
Jennifer Cuney
Ava Dahlstrom
Carl J. Dalio
Eric Dalio
James Daniels
Robert G. Datson
Philip Davis
Donald W. DeCoster
Janet Delaney
Joanne Delude
Lawrence Depenbusch
Kimberly Devore
Douglas Dick
Dalas Disney
MaryJane Donovan
Petr Dostal
Mary Claire Downing
Michael Driscoll
Catherine Dunn
Diane Durane
Douglas Eichelberger
Michael Eltrich
Annette English
Brian Erickson
Kristine K. Ewoldt
Carolyn S. Fedler
Ray Fedler
Curtis Worth Fentress
Coleen Fisher
Cydney Fisher
Margaret Fisher
Robert Fitzgerald
Josephine Flanagan
Ellen Flynn-Heapes
Lewis Fowler
Frank Fritz
Steven Fritzky
Peter Frothingham
Lisa K. Fudge

Marie Fulop
J. Scott Gabel
John Gagnon
Marjorie A. Gallion
Kathleen Corner Galvin
Michael Gengler
Haia Ghalib
Linda Ghannam
Gregory R. Gidez
Karen Gilbert
Mitchell Lee Gilbert
Dawn Givens
Edward Goewert
Ken Goff
Mitchell Gomez
David Goorman
Roxanne Gorrell
John Gossett
Stanley Gould
Jean L. Greaves
Randy Green
Stephen O. Gregory
Robert C. Grubbs
Gregory J. Guastella
D'Anne Gudeman
Renata Hajek
Kristin Halstrum
Christie Halverson-
    Larson
Elizabeth Hamilton
Timothy Hanagan
Mark T. Harpe
Frederic M. Harrington
Geoffrey B. Harris
Milan Hart
James F. Hartman
William Haskey
Ala F. Hason
Frank G. Hege
JoAnne Hege
Michael Henry
Richard A. Herbert
Sheryl Highsmith
Erin Hillhouse
Bridget Hilton
Kimble Hobbs
Barbara K. Hochstetler
Warren Hogue, III
Kimberly J. Holmes
Brian Homerding
Jon Hooley
Laurie Horn
Ernest W. Howard
Arthur A. Hoy, III
June Huhn
Doris Hung
Kelly Hynes
Lisa Jelliffe

Charles Johns
Kelly J. Johnson
Lynn Wisecarver Johnson
Greg Jones
Glenda Jordan
Judith Jump
J. Mike Klebba
Anthia Kappos
Jeff M. Kaufman
Kathy Diane Kavan
Jeffrey Keast
Andrew Kelmers
Nancy Kettner
Michael Kicklighter
Earl John Kincaid
Angeline C. Kinnaird
Ned Kirschbaum
Mary Jane Koenig
Loretta Konrad
Kathleen Krenzer
John M. Kudrycki
Stan Kulesa
Barbara Kusske
Rene L. Lancaster
Bere Lane
Lauren Lee
Linda Lee
Greg Lemon
Leslie Leydorf
Forrest A. Liles
Robert Louden
Harold O. Love
Christoph B. Lueder
Randy E. Macmillan
Robin Mahaffey
Renee Major
Colleen Marcus
John L. Mason
Karin Mason
Sally Mason
John K. McCauley
Carla L. McConnell
John M. McGahey
Loren McGlone
Patrick M. McKelvey
Daniel F. McLaughlin
Geeta Mehta
Julia Mendelson
David Miller
Michael Miller
Pam Mills
Francis Mishler
Doni Mitchell
Mona Mohney
Daniel L. Monger
Wilbur Moore
Gary Morris
Ned Morris

Bruce R. Mosteller
Jack M. Mousseau
Rodney Mowry
Jacqueline Murray
Richard D. Myers
Dan Naegele
Sonja Natter
James Niemi
Minh (Mark) Nguyen
Kathy Nightengale
Lyn K. Oda
Marnie Odegard
Clement Okoye
A. Chris Olson
Christian Olson
Jeff Olson
Brian Ostler
Kathy O'Donnell
Robert J. O'Donnell
James W. O'Neill
Teri Paris
Michel Pariseau
Wee Park
Wendy Paulson
Beverly G. Pax
Frederick R. Pax
John Petro
W. Harrison Phillips
Elisabeth Post
Dorothy Potter
Gary Prager
Brit Probst
Sandy Prouty
Gerard Prus
Clay Pryor
Michelle Ray
Robert Reedy
Heather Richardson
Sherri Riepe
Shannon Riley
Penelope Roberts
Blaine Rodgers
David Robb
Brigette Rothfuss-Moore
Robert Root
William Rosebrook
Lou Ann Roses
Tim Roush
Raymond L. Rupert
Alexander S. Ryou
Janice M. Sadar
Robin Sakahara
John M. Salisbury
Carol Scheibe
Laura M. Schumacher
Stuart A. Schunck
Anthony F. Serratore
Lisa Shelton

Jyh-Lin Michael Shen
Aleksandr Sheykhet
Catherine Shields
Harold T. Small
Carol Ann Smith
Jill Smith
Jim Snyder
Amy Solomon
Joseph Solomon
Jessica Sommers
Christy Sorrese
Joy Spatz
Eric A. Spielman
John J. Stein
Byron Stewart
Maggie Stienstra
Carolyn S. Stojeba
Donald Strum
Les Stuart
Leslie Sudders
Voraporn (Mai)
    Sundarupura
Randy Swanson
Nathaniel A. Taiwo
John R. Taylor
Thomas P. Theobald
Debbie Thurgood
David Tompkins
Chris Tons
Samuel Tyner
Virginia Valocchi
Karen E. Volton
Mark A. Wagner
Thomas J. Walsh
Patricia Walton
Chris Weber
Kristen Wehrli
Dave B. Weigand
Neil Weigert
Richart T. Weldon
Dale White
Marilyn White
Deanna Williams
Catherine Wilson
Michael O. Winters
Michael Wisneski
Lynda Woodhall
Wendy Woodhall
Kevin Wright
John C. Wurzenberger, Jr.
Jun Xia
John S. Yanz
Ivy Yau
Mark Young
Robert Young
Billy F. Zamora
Anna M. Zemko
Monica Zorens

AWARDS

**1994 FIRM OF THE YEAR, COLORADO CHAPTER OF
THE AMERICAN INSTITUTE OF ARCHITECTS**

WINNING DESIGN COMPETITIONS

1990 Colorado Convention Center, Denver, Colorado

1992 Clark County Government Center, Las Vegas, Nevada

1992 National Cowboy Hall of Fame, Oklahoma City, Oklahoma

1992 Natural Resources Building, Olympia, Washington

1992 New Seoul Metropolitan Airport, Seoul, Republic of Korea

NATIONAL CITATIONS

American Institute of Architects
1990 Citation for Excellence, Architecture for Justice Exhibition,
Jefferson County Government Center

1993 Award of Citation, American Association of School Administrators,
Gemmill Mathematics Library and Engineering Sciences Building

SELECTED AWARDS

Western Mountain Region of the American Institute of Architects
1984 Award of Merit, Odd Fellows Hall

1985 Award of Honor, 1999 Broadway

1985 Award of Honor, Museum of Western Art

1986 Award of Merit, One DTC

1989 Award of Excellence in Architecture, Denver Permit Center

1990 Award of Merit, Colorado Convention Center

1991 Award of Merit, Black American West Museum

1991 Award of Honor, Jefferson County Human Services Building

1991 Award of Merit, Ronstadt Transit Center

1994 Award of Honor, Denver International Airport

Colorado Chapter of the American Institute of Architects
1984 Design Award, Museum of Western Art

1985 Design Award, Odd Fellows Hall

1989 Award of Merit, Denver Permit Center

1990 Award of Merit, 1999 Broadway

1990 Award of Honor, Colorado Convention Center

1992 Design Award, Kittredge Building

1994 Award of Honor, Denver International Airport

Northern Colorado Chapter of the American Institute of Architects
1992 Design Award, Leanin Tree Gallery

Denver Chapter of the American Institute of Architects
1985 Award of Honor, Museum of Western Art

1985 Award of Honor, Best of Show, Museum of Western Art

1987 Award of Honor, Museum of Western Art

1988 Award of Merit, Odd Fellows Hall

1991 Award of Merit, Black American West Museum

1991 Award of Honor, Colorado Convention Center

1991 Award of Merit, Denver Permit Center

1991 Award of Merit, Jefferson County Human Services Building

1991 Award of Merit, Ronstadt Transit Center

1994 Award of Honor, Denver International Airport

1994 Award of Merit, Gemmill Mathematics Library and Engineering
Sciences Building

**Kansas Society of Architects of the American Institute
of Architects**
1990 Award of Honor, Museum of Western Art

Portland Chapter of the American Institute of Architects
1993 Award of Merit, Architecture and Energy, Natural Resources
Building

COMMUNITY AWARDS

1981 Young Professional of the Year, *Building Design & Construction
Magazine.*

1985 Ten Most Distinguished, *Denver Business Magazine.*

1990 Award of Achievement, Professional Engineers of Colorado.

1991 Interior Design Giant, *Interior Design Magazine.*

1991 Architect of the Year, American Subcontractors Association of
Colorado.

SELECTED BIBLIOGRAPHY

"Architecture and energy building excellence in the northwest: 1993 Design Awards." *Architecture* 82, no. 5 (May 1993): 113.

Arnaboldi, Mario Antonio. "Airport on the Water." *l'Arca* 71 (May 1993): 24–29.

Berger, Horst. "Modern Basilica." *Fabrics in Architecture* 5, no. 3 (May–June 1993): 10–21.

Brown, Daniel C. "Reviving an architectural pioneer." *Building Design and Construction* 24, no. 10 (October 1983): 40–43.

"C.W. Fentress and Associates: Denver landmark: Odd Fellows Hall." *Interiors* 142, no. 9 (April 1983): 22.

"C.W. Fentress designs Denver's Reliance Center." *Architectural Record* 170, no. 4 (March 1982): 41.

Canty, Donald. "Building with a checkered past renovated as a museum." *Architecture* 75, no. 11 (November 1986): 78–79.

Cattaneo, Renato. "A canopied air terminal." *l'Arca* 73 (July–August 1993): 19–23.

Chalmers, Ray. "Mullion-free exterior enhances office views: Four-sided structural silicone glazing first in the Rocky Mountain Region." *Building Design and Construction* 25, no. 3, (March 1984): 176–79.

Chandler, Roger A. "Learning from Las Vegas? The Clark County Government Center." *Competitions* 2 (Winter 1992): 31–39.

———. "Variations on a theme: Americans win airport competitions on the Pacific rim." *Competitions* 3 (Summer 1993): 30–39.

Cohen, Edie. "Curtis Fentress, the architect restricts intervention in an historically significant Denver house." *Interior Design* 65, no. 4 (March 1994): 112–15.

"Convention center offers dramatic design." *Sun Coast Architect–Builder*, 56, no. 11 (November 1991): W sect., pp. 28–30.

Cooper, Jerry. "Balboa Company: Fifty-seven floors above the Mile-High City, C.W. Fentress and Associates creates art-inspired corporate offices for a Denver investor." *Interior Design* 58, no. 10 (August 1987): 188–92.

"Curtis Worth Fentress." *Denver Business Journal*, 13, no. 4 (December 1985): 23.

Della Corte, Evelyn. "The Museum of Western Art: The interiors of Denver's newest museum win 1984 ASID project design award." *Interior Design* 55, no. 10 (October 1984): 204–9.

"Denver airport design unveiled: The terminal will be capped by one of the nation's largest cable supported fabric roofs." *Building Design and Construction* 32, no. 1 (January 1991): 17.

"Denver Permit Center, Denver, Colorado." *New Mexico Architecture* 31, no. 3–4, May–August 1990: 17.

"Denver: Take a closer look." *Fortune* 127, no. 8 (April 19, 1993): 164–72.

Dietsch, Deborah K. "Green realities: Architects must agree on standards to distinguish the green from the faux." *Architecture* 83, no. 6 (June 1993): 15.

Eng, Rick. "1999 Broadway establishes harmony between skyscraper and sanctuary." *Designers West*, 33, no. 6 (April 1986): 86–87.

Fentress, Curtis Worth. "Architect explains design goals of new Colorado Convention Center." *Denver Post* June 18, 1990, B7.

———. "Convention center took its model from future." *Rocky Mountain News* June 18, 1990, 44.

———. "Design intelligence." *Sun Belt Buildings Journal* 9, no. 12 (April 1985): 7.

———. "Doughnut hole can coexist in city plan." *Rocky Mountain News* April 30, 1983, N32.

———. "Preservation requires skill." *Rocky Mountain News* January 31, 1984, B29.

——— and Richard Weingardt. "One Denver Tech Center: Commanding views of earth and sky." *Modern Steel Construction* 27, no. 6 (November–December 1987): 23–27.

Fisher, Thomas. "Projects: Flights of fantasy." *Progressive Architecture* 73, no. 3 (March 1992): 105–7.

"Frankly speaking: Curt Fentress and Jim Bradburn talk about the practice of architecture." *Daily Journal* 94, no. 44 (July 24, 1990): sect. 2, pp. 11–12.

Hardenbaugh, Don, comp. *Retrospective of Courthouse Design 1980–1991*. Williamsburg, Va: National Center for State Courts, 1992, 64–65.

Harriman, Marc S. "Designing for daylight." *Architecture* 81, no. 10 (October 1992): 89.

Henderson, Justin. "Convening comfortably: C.W. Fentress J.H. Bradburn and Associates humanize the overscale in the new Colorado Convention Center." *Interiors* 150, no. 12 (July 1991): 44–49.

———. "For the People: Accessibility inspires the master plan for the Jefferson County Municipal Center by C.W. Fentress J. H. Bradburn and Associates." *Interiors* 150, no. 12 (July 1991): 50–51.

"How an unusual site influenced architecture." *Building Design and Construction* 21, no. 10 (October 1980): 56–57.

"International design competition: The New Seoul Metropolitan Airport Passenger Terminal." *Architecture and Environment* no. 101, (January 1993): 123–71.

"Jefferson County Human Services." *Progressive Architecture* 74, no. 3 (March 1993): 42–43.

Kania, Alan. "C.W. Fentress J.H. Bradburn and Associates celebrating ten-year anniversary." *Daily Journal* 94, no. 44, (July 24, 1990): sect. 2, pp. 1–2.

Landecker, Heidi. "Airport departures." *Architecture* 82, no. 8 (August 1993): 42–45.

Loebelson, Andrew. "The second 100 interior design giants of 1991." *Interior Design* 62, no. 10 (July 1991): 49–64.

Maluga, Mark J. "Denver Permit Center: Fast-track facelift classically revitalizes a 1960's structure." *Building Design and Construction* 31, no. 11 (November 1990): 62–65.

"A new financial center in Tucson draws on the mission style." *Interiors* 146, no. 4 (November 1986): 40.

"New Seoul Metropolitan Airport." *Progressive Architecture* 74, no. 3 (March 1993): 25.

Oliszewicz, B. Ann. "Young professionals competition." *Building Design and Construction* 21, no. 10 (October 1980): 54–55.

"Olympia's Natural Resources Building." *Architectural Record* 178, no. 12 (November 1990): 15.

"On the boards: Natural Resources Building, Olympia, Washington. C.W. Fentress J.H. Bradburn and Associates." *Architecture* 80, no. 5 (May 1991): 48.

"On the horizon, Denver architects and their work: C.W. Fentress." *Colorado Homes and Lifestyles* 5, no. 2 (March–April 1985): 42–45.

"Pencil Points: Shades of Saint Barts." *Progressive Architecture* 64, no. 10 (October 1983): 49.

Pierson, John. "Denver airport rises under gossamer roof." *Wall Street Journal* 127, no. 99 (November 17, 1992): Western Edition, B1.

"Projects: Flights of fantasy." *Progressive Architecture* 73, no. 3 (March 1992): 105–6.

"Projects in progress." *Sun Coast Architect–Builder* 47, no. 8 (August 1982): 26.

Rebeck, Gene. "Monumental potential." *Fabrics in Architecture* 4, no. 4 (July–August 1992): 16.

"Restoration revives architectural character yet permits modern styling." *Sun Coast Architect–Builder* 53, no. 5 (May 1988): 38–39.

Russell, James S. "Height + Water = Cool." *Architectural Record* 180, no. 8 (August 1992): 40–41.

"Saving grace: The survival of Holy Ghost Church in Denver, Colorado is secured by development." *Interiors* 141, no. 10 (May 1982): 22.

Shaman, Diane. "Seeking remedies for indoor air pollution problems." *New York Times*, April 12, 1992, sect. 1, pp. 0, 13.

"Sloped terraces for an office building in Denver, Colorado." *L'Industria Italiana del Cemento* 651 (January 1991): 38–46.

Stein, Karen D. "Snow-capped symbol." *Architectural Record* 181, no. 6 (June 1993): 106–107.

"Thin sheets of air." *Progressive Architecture* 66, no. 6 (June 1985): 104–10.

"Transit Center provides oasis of comfort for bus passengers." *Sun Coast Architect–Builder* 58, no. 5 (May 1993): W2–W3.

"Tucson bank tower suggests influence of Spanish missions." *Buildings Design Journal* 3, no. 9 (September 1985): 8.

Walker, Diane N. ed. *American Architecture, the state of the art in the 80's.* Ashland, Ky: Hanover Publishing Company, 1985. 10–11, 132–33.

Weingardt, Richard. "Colorado architecture: The best buildings of the modern age." *Colorado Business Magazine* 17, no. 2 (February 1990): 38–43.

——— and Jeff Rundles. "Magnificent Colorado structures never built." *Colorado Business Magazine* 19, no. 2 (February 1992): 41–44.

"Young Jong Island: New international airport design competition." *Architectural Culture* 140 (January 1993): 204–13.

CREDITS

PHOTOGRAPHS

Paul Abdoo, 216, 217, 218

Architectural Forum, 17:6

© Art Institute of Chicago, Chicago, Illinois, 16:1, 16:3, 18:13, 30:3

© Art Resource, New York, New York; Bridgeman, 10:3; Giraudon, 10:2; SEF, 10:1

Patrick Barta, 137:middle, 138, 139:top

Gary Benson; Comstock Stock Photography, 190:top

Tom Bonner, 20:19

Ron Booth, 172:bottom right

Jerry Butts, 56, 206:7, 207:6, 208:5

© C.W. Fentress J.H. Bradburn and Associates, PC., 21:28, 22:30, 45, 60, 75, 82

Cabanban, 40, 41, 43, 204:2

© Chicago Historical Society, 16:2

Cincinnati Historical Society, Cincinnati, Ohio, 23:36

Martin Cole, 21:23, 44, 46, 48, 55:bottom, 57, 205:5, 207:2, 208:2

© Colorado Springs Fine Arts Center, Colorado, Springs, Colorado; Bill Bowers, 12:13

Ed Cooper, 176:middle right

Larry Davenport, 212:5

© Denver International Airport, Public Relations Office, Denver, Colorado, 12:17, 211:5

Denver Public Library, Western History/Geneology Department, Denver, Colorado, 11:10, 22:31

© Esto; Peter Aaron, 21:26; Scott Frances, 17:7, 33:12; Jock Pottle, 23:35; Ezra Stoller, 19:18, 30:4, 31:5

Frank Lloyd Wright Foundation; © The Frank Lloyd Wright Archives, 18:11, 18:12, 23:37

T.S. Gordan, 12:15, 54, 55:top, 204:4, 205:3, 205:7, 207:3

© Hedrich-Blessing, 20:21; Nick Merrick, 12:14, 12:18, 14:frontispiece, 21:25, 21:27, 22:29, 22:33, 22:34, 23:38, 24:41, 24:44, 25:45, 25:47, 36, 37, 39, 47, 49, 50, 51, 58, 59, 61, 63, 64:left, 65, 66, 67, 69, 70, 71, 74, 76, 77, 78, 79, 80, 81, 88, 89, 90, 91, 92, 93, 94, 95, 98, 99, 101, 106, 107, 108, 109, 110, 111, 112, 113, 114, 115, 116, 117, 120, 121, 122, 123, 129, 130, 131, 132, 133, 135, 136, 137:top, 139:bottom, 149, 152, 153, 154, 155, 185, 204:6, 204:8, 206:3, 207:1, 209:5, 209:6, 209:8, 210:2, 210:4, 211:3, 211:6, 212:1, 212:2; Jon Miller, 19:17, 83, 206:6, 209:3, 209:4

Arthur A. Hoy, III, 176:bottom left, 176:bottom right, 211:1

Timothy Hursley, 17:5, 24:39, 24:40, 28:frontispiece, 32:9, 33:13, 64:right, 102, 103, 140, 141, 142, 143, 148, 150, 151, 156, 157, 158, 159, 174, 175, 177, 179, 210:3

© Franz Jantzen, 25:46

John Fitzgerald Kennedy Library, Boston, Massachussetts, 20:22

Ron Johnson, 12:19, 12:20, 21:24, 24:42, 24:43, 31:7, 33:14, 68:left top, 68:left middle, 68:left bottom, 100, 165, 170, 171, 173, 180, 181, 184, 188, 189, 196, 197, 200:bottom, 201:top right, 205:6, 208:1, 208:6, 209:1, 209:7, 210:5, 211:2, 212:3, 212:5, 214:2, 214:3, 214:4, 214:6, 215:4

William Lesch, 73, 208:3

Thorney Lieberman, 12:16, 124, 125, 128, 176:top, 177, 214:1

Norman McGrath, 18:15

Kevin O. Mooney, 16:4

© Museum of Modern Art, New York, New York, 15:frontispiece; Mies van der Rohe Archive, 19:16

© Norman Foster and Associates; John Donat, 20:20

© North Carolina State Fair, Raleigh, North Carolina, 30:1

© North Carolina State University at Raleigh, Design Research and Service, School of Design, 30:2

Office of Cultural Properties, Ministry of Culture and Information, Seoul, Korea; Kim Dae-byuk, 9:frontispiece

Michael Peck, 207:7

© Pei Cobb Freed and Partners, Architects; Steve Rosenthal, 18:14

Jock Pottle, 53, 54

Peter Powles, 17:9

Robert Reck, 17:8

St. Louis Convention and Visitor's Commission, St. Louis, Missouri, 31:6

© St. Paul's Chapel, Colorado, Springs, Colorado; Bob McIntyre, 12:11

© Skidmore Owings and Merrill; Image Source, Inc., 17:10

Smith and LaCasse, 206:5

Bob Springate, 84, 85

© Stock Imagery; James Frank, 176:middle left; Kent Knudson, 192:bottom left; Francie Manning, 190:bottom; M&J Miller, 172:bottom left; Chris Rogers, 192:bottom right

Jim Thompson, 204:1, 204:3, 205:2, 205:4

© University of California at Santa Barbara, University Art Museum, Architectural Drawing Collection, 11:8; Fred Dapperich, 11:7; Dr. David Gebhard, 11:5; F.W. Geisler, 11:6; Willard Morgan, 11:9; Stevens and Cobb, 10:4

© University of Colorado at Boulder; Ken Abbott, 12:12

Wayne Thom Associates, 204:7, 207:4, 207:5, 208:4

Roger Whitacre, 22:32, 29:frontispiece, 210:1

ILLUSTRATIONS

Brian Chaffee, 181:bottom, 184:bottom

Carl J. Dalio, 8:frontispiece, 166, 167, 168, 169, 172, 178, 183:top, 186, 187, 191, 198, 199, 200, 201, 205:1, 206:1, 206:4, 208:7, 209:2, 211:4, 213:1, 213:2, 213:4, 213:7, 214:5, 215:2, 215:3, 215:5

Carlos Denise, 205:8

Stan Doctor, 162, 163, 192, 193, 194, 195, 210:6, 210:7, 213:6, 215:1

Curtis Worth Fentress, 42:bottom, 60, 67, 72, 78:top, 82:bottom left, 87:top, 97:bottom right, 104:left, 118:bottom, 120:top, 134:bottom left, 144, 170:bottom left, 174:bottom left, 186:bottom left, 194:bottom, 200:bottom left

John Gossett, 213:3

Frederick R. Pax, 206:2

Michael O. Winters, 212:4